2 BOOKS IN

THE HOUSEPLANT GUIDE

FOR BEGINNERS AND PLANT LOVERS

A comprehensive book to choose,
grow and live better with your indoor plants

THE HOUSEPLANT BOOK

FOR BEGINNERS

The Best Plants to Grow Indoors for Plant Lovers
and Aspiring Green Thumbers.
The Simple Guide To Choose the Right Plant for You.

CHRISTO SULLIVAN

A COMPREHENSIVE BOOK TO CHOOSE, GROW AND LIVE BETTER WITH YOUR INDOOR PLANTS

THE HOUSE PLANTS GUIDE

FOR **BEGINNERS** AND **PLANT LOVERS**

CONTENTS

FOREWORD

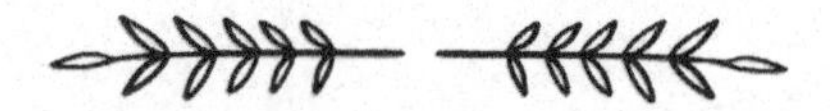

Welcome to the extraordinary world of making your house a better, more natural and healthier place!

Today's urban life is so hectic and the experience of life has become so prominent with this world's latest events, that having plants friends in our homes help us to stop, take a breath and relax. They bring into our houses that contact with Mother Nature that we often easily forget, but that is with us, humans, since the dawn of time. Nature was our home!

Me, I'm an old guy. I retired from the bustle and hustle of the city a long time ago, as I was fortunate enough to part early enough from society with no need to ever look back.[1] Since then, I've been living with my family and my best friends surrounded by green hills, and enjoying every single day.

But enough of me. This book is about those friends of mine.

Those friends are green - mostly. Some with big leaves, some with long and sleek ones. Some I keep in my garden, some in containers, in and outside my porch. And some of them, I keep them inside my house, and they give back as much love as they are given.

This book is a practical guide about plants that you can keep inside you house. How, why and where.

---

[1] *One day I might be even writing about how I achieved such freedom.*

I've tried to enclose in this guide 17 years of experience and love for the greenies. They are strictly results of my opinions and personal tastes, what I tried worked with many trials and errors. Each and every plant though is talking to you, if you know how to listen to her. So you are free to add your own experience to what hopefully you will learn in these pages. **Let's begin.**

INTRODUCTION

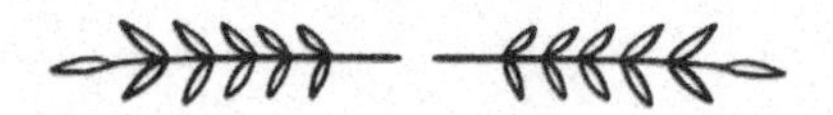

The best houseplants, whether in a residential or business environment, will help make both spaces seem more radiant than you regular home or office. There are several popular houseplants that naturally exude their elegance through their scent, color, form, and size variations, which can help make a space appear more welcoming when viewed.

What we are used to consider common house plants often have unique requirements, such as watering and lighting requirements. Raising our green buddies is simple, but we should make use of some shrewdness and precautions to make them thrive. We will go through each and every step necessary for that to happen.

However, before knowing how to provide these plants with the care they need, we first need to determine which houseplants are best for us, our environment, and why not our mood.

By definition a houseplant is raised indoors, but that doesn't mean that some of them exclusively belong to the indoors realm. Some plants that you would expect to see in your garden can embellish also the interiors of our homes, think for instance about the English Ivy, the Boston Fern, or the Areca Palm.

We'll see how indoor houseplants also helps us to keep the air clear and supply more oxygen to the closed environment of the house. Having some of these plants at home is potentially beneficial to one's wellbeing because they help to filter toxins from the air (toxins such carbon monoxide and ammonia). Not just that: some houseplants can also aid humans avoid developing diseases by reducing the amount of moisture and dust particles in the air, and the healthier the plant is, the more it can help us living healthier.

Another fact that I've always found amusing about some plants is their ability to prosper also in low-light environments (thus the term "low-light houseplants"). However, it is better to never confine them in areas where there are no light sources at all. These plants will also need some sunlight, the level of which will depend on few variables.

If you believe you've never had a "green thumb", then it's time to thing you've got green hands, put some dirt on them and not just aiming to keep them alive. Let's make them happy!

These living creatures, it turns out, can do far better for your physical and emotional health than they can for your living room furniture, as shown by modern findings In fact, houseplants are beneficial to your wellbeing in addition to their aesthetic value.

Why? Well, we all have studied it in our school years: the chlorophyll photosynthesis. To refresh your memory, this is the process in which they do the exact reverse of what we do when we breathe: they emit oxygen and absorb carbon dioxide.

This not only means that they clean the air, but also that they removes toxic chemicals. According to a NASA study, houseplants will kill up to 87 percent of air toxin in a room in just 24 hours.

Let me tell you a secret: I adore it when people are ecstatic or enthusiastic to get and raise a plant in their home, particularly if they were unsuccessful the first time. It means they're ready to try again, which is all life is about after all. Maybe this time they'll be more tuned in to their silent, green friend.

You will learn about the best plants to start with, how to care for them, and how to diagnose and handle common problems. But most importantly, I hope that the more that you'll learn the more that you will realize you love them. Once you do, you're half-way there.

CHAPTER ONE

Benefits of Houseplants

Any interior should have at least one houseplant. Greenery brightens up indoor spaces and is believed to improve one's mood. Houseplants are common because they are simple to care for, provide health benefits, and can be used to complement a number of interior design projects. Indoor plants are a perfect choice for people who don't have enough yard space for an outdoor garden or who live in areas where the winters are bitterly cold.

- **HOUSEPLANTS MAKES BREATHING EASIER**

Your body takes in oxygen and exhales carbon dioxide as you breathe. Plants absorb carbon dioxide and emit oxygen during photosynthesis. Plants and humans are natural partners because of their opposing gas use patterns. Increased oxygen levels can be achieved by adding plants to interior spaces. Photosynthesis stops at night and plants breathe like humans, consuming oxygen and releasing carbon dioxide. On the other hand, other plants do exactly the opposite! Orchids, succulents, and epiphytic bromeliads and Areca Palms, for example, absorbs carbon dioxide and releasing oxygen at night. Isn't it magical? Place these plants in bedrooms to help you sleep well at night.

- **HOUSEPLANTS HELP PURIFY AIR**

According to NASA reports, plants extract up to 87 percent of volatile organic compounds (VOCs) from the environment every 24 hours. Formaldehyde (found in rugs, vinyl, tobacco smoke, and shopping bags), benzene, and trichloroethylene are examples of VOCs (both found in man-made fibers, inks, solvents and paint). Benzene is typically present in high quantities in research areas, where there are several books and printed journals.

VOCs are trapped inside modern climate-controlled, air-tight homes. Plants purify trapped air by drawing pollutants into the soil, where root zone microorganisms turn VOCs into food for the plant, according to this NASA study[2].

Houseplants are probably the best natural air purifiers around. They can remove harmful chemicals like formaldehyde and benzene from the air, substances often used in paint, cigarettes, vinyl, and solvents.

- **HOUSEPLANTS ARE NATURAL HUMIDIFIERS**

Plants emit moisture vapour as part of their photosynthetic and respiratory cycles, raising the humidity of the air surrounding them. Plants expel about 97 percent of the water they consume. When you place multiple plants together, the temperature in the room rises, which helps to keep respiratory problems at bay. Weak skin, colds, sore throats, and dry coughs are all reduced as plants are used in indoor spaces. Plants can be a great aid during winters, because they increase the humidity in the air by releasing water as moisture vapour, which can help us avoid breathing issues.

If you are in any way like me, try to place a few Boston Ferns around your home instead of spending money on a pricey appliance to control dry winter weather. They expel moisture by a mechanism known as transpiration, in which the pores on the underside of the leaves sweat and release much-needed moisture.

---

[2] *https://ntrs.nasa.gov/citations/19930073077*

• HOUSEPLANTS CAN REDUCE STRESS

Do you suffer from work-related stress? Experts suggest keeping potted plants near your desk to reduce discomfort and exhaustion. Plants in workplaces have been shown to help people's pulse rates, blood pressure, and respiratory problems, according to studies. This is why it's a good idea to keep potted plants near your desk because they can relieve tension and anxiety, allowing you to function more efficiently.

Working with plants close by, according to the researchers, can help with both physiological and psychological tension. Plants in the office, or at home, will help you feel more relaxed, soothed, and more in tune with nature, according to a study published in the Journal of Physiological Anthropology[3].

Participants in the study were assigned one of two tasks: repotting a houseplant or performing a brief computer-based task. The biological factors associated with stress, such as heart rate and blood pressure, were assessed during each project.

They discovered that the stress response in the subjects was reduced when they were given an indoor gardening mission. The computer project, on the other hand, resulted in an increase in heart rate and blood pressure, despite the fact that the research subjects were young men who were used to working with computers.

• HOUSEPLANTS HAVE HEALING POWERS

Many plants have soothing properties; Aloe Vera, for example, was known in ancient Egypt as the "plant of immortality" and was used to

---

3 *https://jphysiolanthropol.biomedcentral.com/articles/10.1186/s40101-015-0060-8*

treat wounds. We nowadays use it to relieve pain from sunburns or burns. Rooms with plants often contain less pollen and mould than rooms without any leaves, according to the researchers. Allergens and other airborne contaminants are caught by the leaves and other parts of the plants, which serve as natural filters.

• HOUSEPLANTS SOOTHE EYES

When your eyes are sore or drained (perhaps after hours in front of a computer), many people think that all you have to do is look at a Pothos plant to alleviate eye strain. It's also thought to protect against glaucoma and cataracts.

• HOUSEPLANTS GIVE HEALTHY PRODUCE

It is not uncommon to grow fruit and vegetables indoors. Many individuals, from those with rooftop gardens to those with window gardens, have already done so. You not only save money by not having to buy food at the store, but you also know that everything that grows in your indoor garden is new and pesticide-free!

• **HOUSEPLANTS CAN HELP YOU SLEEP BETTER**

The advantages of including indoor plants in your home go beyond avoiding respiratory problems and mitigating stress. When put in your bedroom, indoor plants such as Jasmine, Lavender, Aloe Vera, and Gardenia will improve the quality of your sleep. These plants have a gentle calming effect on the body and mind, which can help to reduce heart rate, blood pressure, and tension. It also lowers anxiety levels, resulting in a healthier mood and sleep quality.

• **HOUSEPLANTS CAN HELP FIGHT COLDS**

The potential of plants to humidify the air and reduce dust will aid in the battle against viruses that cause colds and coughs. Adding plants to office and hospital environments reduced colds, nausea, headaches, and sore throats, according to several horticulture reports. Some trees, such as eucalyptus, can help to remove congestion from the system.

• **HOUSEPLANTS CAN BE PRETTY HOUSE DECORS**

And let's not forget that nothing says "welcome" like a lovely hanging plant at your front door. Unlike greenhouse plants, most indoor plants need less care; they don't need much irrigation, trimming, or fertilizing. They can also be used to make dish gardens and terrariums in decorative pots. Adding potted plants to different corners of your home's space will also help to create a cool and new atmosphere. You can now turn every inconvenient room into a mini green paradise!

• **HOUSEPLANTS IMPROVE WELLBEING**

A house with plants, of course, seems to be more refreshing than one without. Aside from the fact that their beauty will make you happy, plants are believed to have a close spiritual connection with us. Plants are also present at some of life's most important occasions, such as marriages and funerals.

Patients in hospitals that have a view of a garden have a better chances of healing than those who have a view of a wall or another building, according to studies. Plants add to a greater sense of well-being, making people happier and more positive about life.

Plants in the workplace often reduce nausea, colds, allergies, coughs, sore throats, and flu-like symptoms. In another survey, illness rates in offices with plants, dropped by more than 60%, according to the Agricultural University of Norway[4].

- **HOUSEPLANTS SHARPENS FOCUS**

According to a report conducted at the Royal College of Agriculture in Cirencester, England, students pay 70 percent more attention when they are taught in rooms with plants[5]. Attendance was also higher in lectures held in classrooms with plants, according to the same report.

- **PLANTS MAY BOOST YOUR PRODUCTIVITY**

Bromeliads may be the most helpful coworker you've ever seen. Plants in the workplace have been shown to boost efficiency and innovation in several trials. Students in a campus computer lab performed 12 percent better and were less depressed when plants were located nearby, according to the report.

---

[4] *https://www.peer.de/fileadmin/user_upload/AIRY/AIRY_eFIG_Forschungsergebnisse.pdf*

[5] *https://aplantineveryclassroom.org/research/*

In another study, participants were asked to create imaginative word comparisons. When there was a plant in the room with them, they performed better.

PLANT SELECTION

The 15 Lowest-Maintenance Houseplants for a Healthier Living

If you're new to gardening, here's a list of plants that I feel would be ideal for you. All of them can provide you with plenty of greenery and are simple to maintain. Here are fifteen fantastic indoor plants to help you increase the air quality in your home or apartment.

1. GOLDEN POTHOS

When I was working in an office, the Pothos was dubbed the "cubicle plant" because it was omni-present in most of the desks and working stations. IT is easy to keep, actually it thrives in less-than-ideal conditions. The trailing vines of this plant (like those of the Philodendron), can grow to be over 10 feet long. Benzene, formaldehyde, xylene, and toluene cab be easy filtered by the Pothos.

Pothos is a very popular houseplant that is known for being extremely hard and difficult to destroy. Although Pothos isn't the most efficient air purifier, it's the easiest to care for, so even if you don't have a particularly green thumb, you can be confident it will keep you company for long at home. So if you want the advantages of houseplants but aren't great at keeping them alive ,Pothos is a great place to start!

2. ENGLISH IVY

Ivy is commonly thought of as an outdoor plant that brings rustic beauty to older buildings, but they make great green buddies also at home. Indoors they will help purify your home's air. English ivy is particularly effective at absorbing mould from air: in a study, when

English ivy was placed in a container with moldy bread, it was able to consume a substantial portion of airborne mold[6]. Place it in a sunny spot because this plant prefers bright direct sunshine and slightly dry soil.

3. BOSTON FERN

Here's another easy plant to maintain at home: the Boston ferns. Boston ferns were ranked in NASA's list of air-purifying plants for their ability to remove pollutants such as formaldehyde, plastics, and cigarette smoke from the air. The fern's leaves absorb these substances and convert them into products that the plant can make use of. So if you have a smoker in the family, this one can help to make the envoriment a bit healthier.

4. PEACE LILY

This is one of my wife's favorites! I appreciate their resiliance: the perfect present for someone who neglect his plants (if you really want to give them plants. Don't.): they're very forgiving and will bloom as soon as you give them a pinch of attention. Also the Lili has been discovered by NASA to be effective at removing dangerous compounds in the air. Carbon monoxide, formaldehyde, and benzene are only a few of the chemicals that it can break down.

Peace lilies, also known as "closet plants," do not do well under direct sunlight. Place your peace lily where it can receive indirect light and provide you with all of the advantages of clean air. This is an excellent apartment plant for those who do not have much natural light.

---

6 *https://learn.allergyandair.com/english-ivy-and-mold/*

5. ALOE VERA

The miracle plant! You may already be aware of aloe vera's healing powers: skin-care benefits, sunburn treating, bowel pacifier and many many others. But the best part is that it is very easy to grow, and yes, it can purify our air too. It is especially good in absorbing airborne substances such as paint or cleaning agents.

Aloe vera can also be used in food and beverages, such as juices, and Brownies.

6. SNAKE PLANT

Another outstanding plant to keep home, with a fancy name and look. The thin, upright leaves of this low-maintenance tropical plant have uneven banding that resembles reptile skin. Its drought-resistant structure makes it an ideal plant for anyone, anytime. Not too sensitive, the snake plant can resist weeks even if you forget about it..

CO_2 is absorbed by this plant's seeds, and is then converted to oxygen. This kind of plant is perfect for the bedroom because they boost the air quality while you sleep. Snake plants help to purify the air in your household by removing xylene, toluene, and trichloroethylene.

7. RUBBER PLANT

Looking for a slightly bigger plant to help purify the air in your home? Rubber plants too can withstand a lot of neglect, making them much less difficult to maintain than other plants. Their big leaves accumulate harmful substances from air, which is then converted into nutrients for the plant or compounds for the soil.

8. GERBERA

The Gerbera daisy is hands down the most effective plant in extracting benzene from the environment. According to the Lung Health Institute, gerbera daisies, like snake plants, are precious for their capacity to consume airborne compounds and provide oxygen at night, which can benefit those who suffer from sleep apnea

9. AZALEA

There are just few flowers that can par with an azalea shrub in spring bloom. Choose your own color an embellish your house with this low maintenance plant. Give her some shade and a well-drained soil and she can make any corner of your house special.

Of course also Azaleas can help enhance indoor air quality by removing formaldehyde, in addition to being a lovely flower to add color to your house. Simply remember to spray the azaleas sometimes, as they enjoy a humid environment.

10. MASS CANE

Mass cane, commonly known as corn plant, is a special African plant that works wonders in brightening up an office or home. It's rather peculiar, yet a low-maintenance, slow-growing beauty for those looking for a plant that will look good in their home while still cleaning their air. This is one outhouse plants that without any effort will make you look as a "plant connoisseur". Get it, it's lovely and if you are lucky enough they could even gift you some fragrant white flowers.

11. ZZ PLANT

The ZZ plant is one of the most popular green indoors companions and the gold standard for houseplants beginners. Its peculiar name come from the initial of her original name, Zamioculcas Zamiifolia.

With her waxy smooth leaves, a ZZ Plant is a stunning addition to any low-light environment. They are highly drought resistant and need no upkeep. Moreover, they representprosperity and fellowship, making it an ideal present for any plant lover (or potential plant parent). Just make sure your pet do not chew any of its leaves for they can be toxic.

12. BIRD'S NEST FERN

The fronds of the Bird's Nest Fern have rippled edges and emerge out of a nest-like crown. It makes a lovely indoor hanging vine. Indirect light and a humid atmosphere are ideal for them. Formaldehyde, xylene, and toluene have also been shown to be filtered by ferns. A plant for refined green palates.

13. PHILODENDRON

The Philodendron's heart-shaped leaves and trailing vines can grow to be over 10 feet long in the right indoor conditions, making it an ideal plant for a high shelf. Did I say it's regarded as one of the best houseplants to care for? Formaldehyde is the best substance philodendrons can take care of..

14. SWISS CHEESE PLANT:

A Monstera Deliciosa at home will make you look like a big shot of houseplanting. The particular shapes of the leaves made this plant one of the all-time favorites for houseplants lovers. A 12 inch Monstera is relatively inexpensive and grows easily, so you will have some nice height and leaves in under three months. They require indirect light, especially if you want them to develop their characteristic holes in the leaf.

15. CHLOROPHYTUM COMOSUM (SPIDER PLANT):

The ideal plant if you want to "fill" relatively empty corners or shelf. These are low-maintenance plants that only need weekly watering from the bottom and occasional misting. They produce babies that are easy to reproduce from the tips of their leaves on a regular basis; you will be inundated with baby plants that you can share with friends and relatives!

1. Start slow. The best way to start your journey into house planting is with an easy plant such as those suggested in the suggested plants section of this guide or with a Cactus or Succulent. Succulents and Cacti are often confused since most cacti are classified as succulents. The key distinction is that cacti have areoles, which are bumps from which hair or spikes develop, while succulents do not.

2. Cacti Can Surprise You. Cacti are patient: they can put up with your bad attitudes for years and years before surprising you with flowers until they begin to thrive again. People do not associate cacti with flowers but they are actually capable of beautiful wonders of colors. If well cared for, you have a high chance that your cactus will bloom by their third year. Cacti flourish on fresh growth, which is encouraged by caring for them during the summer and ignoring them during the winter. In addition, when the plant is pot-bound, flowering is often induced. This is a perfect plant to begin with if you're new to holding house plants and they just need a gentle misting of water every now and then.

3. Which brings to our third point. Succulents are perfect first plants. They're absolutely low-maintenance, easy-to-produce, and suitable for most types of homes. They are perfect for windowsills, where they can get the most sunshine. WIth their dense, fleshy leaves and stems, succulents are the best companion to every interior design. Many varieties have rosette-shaped leaves with densely packed leaves, which aid in water conservation in their natural habitat. You could begin with an Echeveria and Sempervivum (houseleek) set, which can provide a fascinating grouping even if no other plants are present, and there are several varieties to select.

4. Never, ever, ever overwater. Most people ruin their houseplants by dumping water down the middle of the plant, giving it much more water than it needs, and simply leaving the water to swamp in the plant since it has nowhere else to go. Excessive stagnant water causes root rot, which eventually kills the vine. If the plant pot has drainage, spray from the bottom with a saucer, or spray daily with an atomizer to help improve the humidity around the plant and keep it happy!

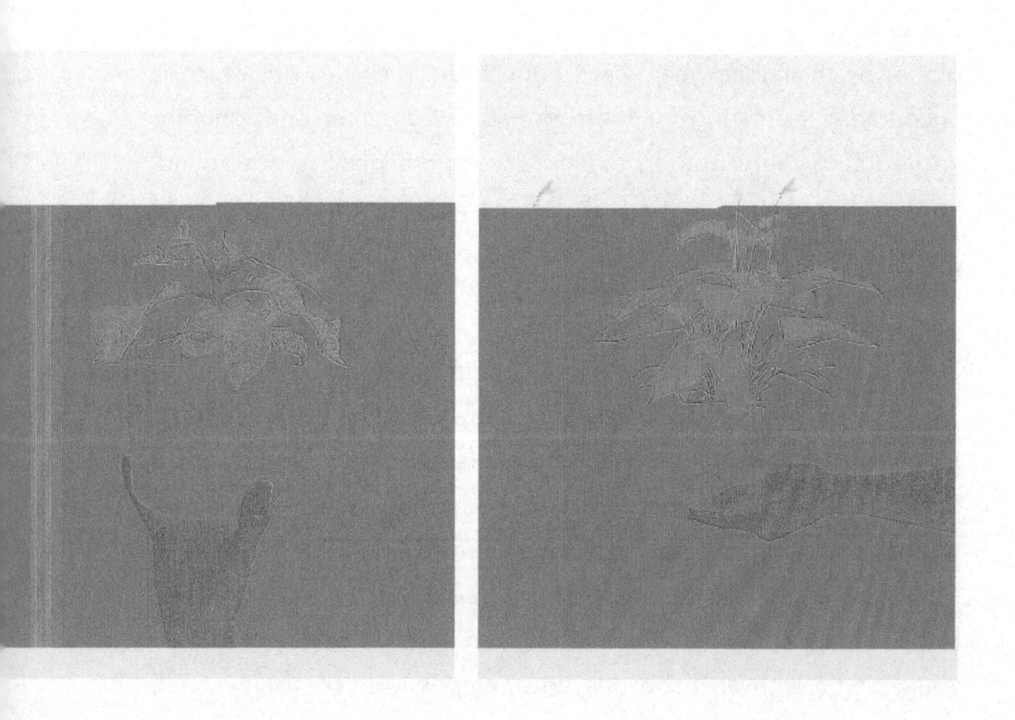

I enjoyed living in the city, but there were times that I wished my apartment had some green space behind it. Especially in the summer, when friends from out of town were committed to tell me how they were creating their raised plant beds, vegetable gardens, and planting fruit trees, berries, and herbs in their yards. I envied because they had the freedom to grow food that they were actually able to feed on. Healthy food thatchy could eat, a dream for my suite-and-tie, go-get-lunch-at-a-supermarket style of life. Until one of my buddies joked about getting myself a garden into my apartment. Well, why not? My first green companion was a plump leaf of Aloe Vera. I loved the mystical proprieties that rumors gave her. Then my first fruit plant was a lemon plant. I've alway been fond of citrus, and I became fond pretty soon of my new plant soon, especially when she started to gift me two wonderful tiny greenish lemons. It felt like magic, and thanks to that first two lemons I now live in a magic wonderland.

So when it comes to growing edible plants in your house, even if you don't have access to a green room, you do have plenty of choices. I'll give you here a list of those plants that by my experience are not challenging to grow and can give you many benefits. Remember that you can also have one or two of those also for decorative reasons, to help clean your indoor air. But most of all I urge you to raise them to use their fruits in your meals: if you're like me, for the first time you will know where your food comes from.

1. AVOCADOS

Avocados are one of today people's favorites. We all know how healthy they can be, and also how good they can taste (if we know how to use them in the kitchen). High in heart-healthy fats; two-thirds of their fat is monounsaturated, which are those fats that can help you lower the risk of cardiovascular diseases and overall mortality. An avocado also has more potassium than a babana, is loaded with fiber and contains a lot of vitamins E and B6, as well as a lot of carotenoids, which have been attributed to a lower risk of cancer. It's no surprise that these fruits are among our favorites.

- How to Grow an Avocado -

It is possible to produce an avocado tree from an avocado pit, but the fruit will not be nutritious, and you may have to wait a long time to enjoy your homegrown avocado toast. The best way to grow your own little avocados is to purchase a dwarf avocado tree if you want to eat what you sow, which is, very conveniently, also the best option to keep it in your house in a sunny spot. There exist varieties that produce larger green-skinned fruits, as well as the more popular black-skinned fruits, which are also excellent.

To care for your tree, fill a big, well-draining pot with sand before filling it with potting mix and planting it. Water it regularly, but make sure the soil is never wet because avocado roots do not like to be damp.

It is recommended to prune the tree's shoots on a regular basis, as is planting the tree in an environment with high ceilings; even dwarf trees can reach heights of more than 10 feet!

- How to Harvest Avocado -

The best part! Green avocados are ready to harvest when the skin turns into a faint yellow color, while darker avocados are ready when the skin turns almost black. If you like them a little more mature, know that ripe fruits can be left on the branches for a few weeks (I suggest not more than two), but if you wait too much the taste and texture of the fruits would begin to deteriorate.

2. LEMONS

My first love! For me it all stared by a little shy lemon plant. It's no secret that lemons are among the healthiest fruit that we can grow from earth. Lemons are high in vitamin C, which aids in the body's collagen synthesis, iron absorption, and protein metabolization. Although it is a spread misconception that big doses of vitamin C will heal the common cold, it is an important food for the immune system.

- How to Grow Lemons -

Get yourself a large pot for this one, to allow the roots of this tree for a good spread. The soil and branches will need to be held moist to simulate a humid environment. To provide your tree with these small caring details, together with adequate watering and nourishment, would result in a freshly perfumed plant that will yield delicious lemons. Sometimes I sit next to my lemon and mandarine trees, I close my eyes, feel the fragrance in the air and imagine myself in a citrus field in the southern part of Italy.

Once again, I recommend to purchase a 2 to 3-year old dwarf tree from a nursery if you want to be able to pick fruits right away. I'm sure that these cute little trees will become also your favorite decorative pride.

So how to go about? First of all choose a clay, ceramic, or plastic pot that is wider than your tree's root ball and has many holes in the rim. Fill the drainage dish with stones to allow air to flow.

Choose a mildly acidic, loam-based potting mix or a potting soil specially designed for citrus trees.

When ready place your tree in a location where it can get 8 to 12 hours of direct sunlight per day and maintains a temperature of 55 to 85 degrees Fahrenheit (about 12 to 30 degrees Celsius).

Don't forget to water on a daily basis, but never overwater the soil. The best indicator is your finger: it should be sticky, not soggy. Also make sure to change the air in the room often and to mist the leaves with a spray bottle on a daily basis to help them stay hydrated.

- How to Harvest Lemons -

You need to wait 6 to 9 months, after which most lemons will ripen. Look for the fullest color and if the rind can be softly squeezed to see if it's ripe. Lemons with a subtle "give" are ready to use in zesty drinks, muffins, main courses, and desserts. Or just to drink in the morning with some water, for a fresh start.

3. MANDARIN ORANGES

Mandarin oranges, my favorite childhood snack. One of the happiest looking trees in the garden, they also make a great addition to any large and bright colored living room. They have a good amount of calcium, vitamin C, and fibers. When you grow your own you will taste the difference with the added syrups one used in canned types.

- How to Grow Mandarin Oranges -

Not many people keep a Mandarin indoor. I promise you it will bring happiness in your household. Maybe it's the green/orange combination, maybe the fragrance... I don't know, but it works, try it.

Growing this tree is very similar to lemons. Buy a dwarf mandarin orange tree, get a large pot with drains at the bottom and fertile soil. They will need to be placed in an area with sun, remember to rotate the plant regularly to ensure that it receives light evenly on all sides. Water it everyday, but wait until the soil is dry before watering again.

Place your tree in a room with a high ceiling, because it can reach 6 feet, as its root system expands with it. You know it's time to repot it when it's too tall, or when you notice the roots starting to expand back o themselves or out the drainage holes. Use a tub or a vase that's at least 2 inches wider in diameter than the root ball.

- How to Harvest Mandarin Oranges -

Harvest mandarins as soon as they turn orange for the best taste. Clip or gently twist and pull the fruit from the tree as they achieve their telltale hue, making sure the "button" at the top of the fruit stays intact.

4. TOMATOES

Who wouldn't like some fresh tomatoes ready to pick? These red, fleshy vegetables are rich of vitamin C and potassium, as well as the antioxidant lycopene, a carotenoid linked to cardiovascular protection.

- *How to Grow Tomatoes* -

Begin by choosing a 6-inch pot for a single plant or a larger pot (approximately 12 inches) for two plants. Start one or two new plants from seed every two weeks to ensure a steady supply of tomatoes.

Pour starter potting mix into the container(s) and plant seeds about 1/4 inch thick. Hold the soil moist but not soggy by watering.

Place the jar in a bright location, rotating the pot(s) every couple of days to ensure that both sides get equal exposure to the sun. In 5 to 10 days, the seeds should germinate.

Transplant the seedlings from the starter mix to potting soil when they are around 3 inches tall. Add an organic fertilizer to the mix about 2 weeks after transplanting.

Water the plant abundantly, always being careful to not get a soggy soil. As the plants get larger you will need to stake them to prevent broken stems.

When the plants are in flower, gently touch the main stem and larger side branches with your finger to facilitate pollination.

- *Tomato Harvesting Techniques* -

Indoor tomatoes don't grow as big as outdoor tomatoes, so don't expect softball-sized fruits. They will most likely be precious pearls full of taste. If you did everything correct they'll have the homegrown tomato flavor (taste will also depends on the kind you'll choose to grow).

You can enjoy the tomatoes as soon as they turn red and solid to the touch, with a subtle "give". Remove the fruits from their stems by clipping or softly twisting and pulling them.

5. GARLIC GREENS

We all need it in our kitchens. One of the healthiest food you could find among your houseplants. A superfood which can reduce blood pressure, has anti-bacterial qualities and can also help reduce breast cancer in specific conditions, Garlic belongs to the allium family. Its pungent smell is worth the benefits.

- *How to Grow Garlic Greens* -

Garlic bulbs are challenging to grow indoors, but garlic greens, which can be used as scallions, are rather simple to grow. They keep garlic's quality while their flavor is a bit more mild, which means you can use also them raw. They're also handy when you want to add a splash of color!

Buy a few garlic bulbs with tiny cloves, and don't be afraid to buy a broken bulb (one that has begun to burst or has fully separated).

Get a 4-inch pot with drainage holes in the bottom, or a quart-size yoghurt tub with holes drilled in the bottom. Have a small bag of potting soil ready.

Fill the pot with soil until it's about half an inch below the surface. Break the bulbs into individual cloves leaving the peel on and press each one into the soil about an inch, with its pointy end up.

Space the cloves about 12 inches apart. Fill the container with water and position it in a sunny location. The soil should be maintained wet but not soggy. After about a week, green shoots should surface.

- How to Harvest Garlic Greens -

Use scissors to clip off whatever you need, just remember to leave around 8 inches of shoots. When the cloves begin to sprout further, compost the contents of the box, re-fill with fresh potting soil, and plant new cloves. Bear to mind that each clove only sprouts healthy greens once; you'll have to keep replanting in order to have a steady supply.

5. CARROTS

Carrots are rich of thiamin, niacin, folate, potassium, and vitamins B6, A, C, and K, among other vitamins and minerals. They also have 3 grammes of fibers per cup, which is a good number.

Carrots take the their name from carotenoids, organic pigments that have antioxidant properties for humans, which they are rich of (like avocados, apricots, asparagus, and broccoli among others).

- How to grow Carrots -

Carrots are one of the best crops to grow indoors due to the ease with which a consistent level of moisture in the soil can be maintained. Carrots can be easily cultivated indoors in a variety of kinds, more types than what you can probably find in your local supermarket. Anyone can grow gorgeous, tasty carrots with only a 12-inch pot, dirt, and a bright window.

Purchase carrot seeds and a 1.5-square-foot pot or window box with the usual drainage holes.

Fill the pot with a humus-rich potting mix to within an inch of the tip. Humus is composed by the organic matter left over after plant and animal matter has decomposed and make a very florid terrain.

Before planting the seeds, water the soil. Plant the seeds in rows 6 inches apart, 1 inch apart, softly pressing them into the soil and covering them with a thin layer of soil.

Put the container somewhere that gets a lot of light. Maintain a wet but not soaked earth. You should soak some peat moss in water overnight and then sprinkle it on top of the seeds to help keep them moist. The seeds should begin sprouting in about 2 weeks.

- *How to Harvest Carrots* -

When the tops of the roots have risen to around 3/4 inch wide - just below the green stem - carrots are ready to harvest. If you can't see the carrot itself, brush away any dirt around the stem to get a better idea of its size.

While I understand that it might be enticing to see how large carrots can grow, once they reach their peak size, they lose their sweetness and taste.

Grab the carrots squarely at the root and wiggle them about a little before pulling straight up. If the soil becomes too hard to harvest, water it and wait an hour or two before trying again. Brush off any extra dirt as soon as the carrots are removed from the soil, and let them dry before storing them in the fridge.

6. SALAD GREENS

There are different kinds of salad greens (iceberg, lettuce, romaine, red leaf, arugula etc.) and most of them are rich of vitamins A, C, and

K, as well as folate and iron, much like microgreens.

- How to Grow Salad Greens -

You can keep in shape with your own salads now, and growing different types and colors of it is a perfect way to liven up otherwise bland salads from a plastic bag. It takes about a month from seed to harvest to get a full plate of salad.

Begin by buying seedlings or starter plants from a nearby nursery (or order seeds online). Fill a planter box with potting soil that has drainage holes in the floor. Poke holes in the soil about 4 inches apart with your finger.

By using seeds, scatter a few in each hole before patting the soil back over the top to cover them. Massage the roots before planting them in a pit and filling in the space surrounding them with soil.

Water the soil after you've planted your seeds. Eradicate all but the biggest, healthiest shoots as soon as they emerge. Water the soil on a daily basis, making sure it's still wet to the touch.

- How to Harvest Salad Greens -

Take off (or clip with scissors) only the outer leaves of mixed greens to allow the plants to continue growing, and be very careful not to damage the roots.

7. MICROGREENS

And the best things in life come in tiny packages: Microgreens. Microgreens are the last healthy food trend. No more shoots and not yet leaves, these superfood seedlings are superstars of any new diet rich in nutrients. They provide more vitamins A,C, K, folate and proteins than their full-grown counterparts. Mix micro greens in a large bowl of mixed greens. Their seeds are available in a range of flavours, including broccoli, cabbage, celery, spinach, mustard, and more.

- How to Grow Microgreens -

Microgreens are tiny green plants that pack a punch in terms of taste and cost in local markets. They are, however, relatively simple to develop at home with a few basic materials, a sunny windowsill, and a small jar. Microgreens will be garnishing your own handmade plates in just 2 - 3 weeks from planting to harvest.

Begin by stocking up on seeds including radishes, kale, Swiss chard, beets, basil, and dill.

Fill a shallow tray (often referred to as a "seedling tray") or a shallow pot with a drainage hole with potting mix and fill to the brim. Using water, moisten the soil until it is humid but not muddy.

Distribute the seeds equally in the soil, they should be close to each other but not touching. Cover the seeds with a thin layer of soil sifted over the top. Lightly sprinkle the dirt with a spray bottle.

Place the tray on a bright windowsill in a room with a temperature range of 60°F (16°C) to 70°F (21°C). Gently spray the soil to keep it moist; don't let it dry out, but don't let it get waterlogged.

The seeds will most likely germinate in 3 to 5 days; once they do, make sure they get 12 to 14 hours of light per day. Keep the soil moist around the roots but not the leaves.

- How to harvest Microgreens -

They're ready to be eaten after the seedlings have risen to a height of 1 or 2 inches (this may take 3 weeks or more) and have around two sets of leaves.

Keep the greens at the stem and cut off the leaves with a pair of scissors, being careful not to cut into the base. Keeping the roots intact will guarantee that your greens can produce several harvests.

Eat the microgreens right away or keep them in the fridge for up to 5 days in a plastic bag. You will love them.

8. SCALLIONS

I always adored them. I may opinion every dish tastes better with a homegrown scallion. Ok, let's call it a fact: any dishes benefit from the inclusion of scallions. They can be grown all year on a sunny windowsill as long as the conditions are perfect.

Scallions, like garlic, belong to the allium genus of vegetables, which has been linked to cancer prevention and can help protect the body from cell-damaging free radicals.

- *How to Grow Scallions* -

Scallions are amazing: they are the simplest vegetable to grow in the kitchen. Simply buy a lot, tie the bulbs in a rubber band, and put the whole bunch (greens, bulbs, and all) in a glass with an inch of water to start rising.

Replace the water on a regular basis. Place the scallions in a shallow pot or other small container until fresh green shoots emerge and the roots have doubled in length (about 7 to 10 days).

Keep the plants in full sun and evenly watered (i.e., don't let the soil get too dry until watering).

- How to Harvest Scallions -

Leave at least an inch or two of the plant in the soil and snip the green tops if required. Harvest the plants until they are 6 inches tall and use the white portion of the scallion. Remove the white clump gently from the soil.

Scallions that have been well washed and cut can be stored in the refrigerator for up to a week. Cover them in a wet paper towel and stack them in a plastic container to keep them safe.

9. CHIVES

The tasty chives! Chives are a quirky little plant that is handy to have on the kitchen counter, ready to be chopped and plopped into your favorite meal. Chives are high in vitamins A and C, as well as phytochemicals that have great antioxidant properties.

- How to Grow Chives -

Since these plants need a little humidity, keep a small dish of pebbles and water nearby to provide the ideal habitat for a safe plant.

Begin by purchasing seeds and a pot with a diameter of 6 to 8 inches. Fill it with potting soil nearly to the top.

Place the jar in a partly shaded area and plant the seeds, making sure they're covered by a thin layer of dirt. Make sure the soil never gets dry by watering it everyday.

- How to Harvest Chives -

Snip leaves from each plant gently, making sure not to cut any of them at once. They are ready for your baked potatoes' toppings.

10. BASIL

The scent of this herb can soothe you and calm everybody around it. The oil eugenol, which can inhibit enzymes in the body that induce swelling, appears to be the source of this flavorful herb's anti-inflammatory properties.

- How to Grow Basil -

When grown indoors, basil can be a fickle plant. It's important to use a waterproof bag to keep the moisture in, as well as pebbles or sand to help drain the dirt. Furthermore, artificial light is important because basil needs a lot of sunlight to produce the best crop.

Begin by ordering seeds or a starter plant from an online retailer, a nursery, or a grocery store.

Make sure to choose a container of at least 4 inches of width and enough drainage holes. Basil prefers mild weather and plenty of sunshine, with at least 6 hours of direct sunlight a day.

Fertilize the soil once a month with organic or slow-release fertilizers like compost tea, and water often, around once a day in extreme heat or every other day in milder weather; the soil should get dry.

Pruning can also help you get the most basil out of your plant. Start cutting back the top leaves as they reach around 6 inches in height. Continue pruning as the plant becomes bushier, pinching off any flowers that emerge.

- Basil Harvesting Instructions -

Snip a few leaves from each plant with a sharp knife whenever you need it. Enjoy some homemade pesto at a moments notice.

11. CILANTRO

More than just enchilada garnish, cilantro contains incredible anti fungal properties and it's a great source vitamin A.

- How to Grow Cilantro -

Growing cilantro indoors can be more challenging than growing it outside, particularly if you are transplanting it from an outdoor spot. Cilantro does not transplant well, start your indoor plant from seeds and use a sandier soil to avoid root rot and nutrient deficiency.

Buy coriander seeds (bet you didn't know: coriander is the seed type of cilantro) or starter plants and choose a jar that's at least 8 inches deep and has drainage holes in the bottom.

Fill the jar halfway with soil, leaving an inch or two of space at the end. Delicately press the seeds into the soil, and water it until it is damp.

Tie plastic wrap around the bag and secure it with rubber bands. After a few days the seedlings should have germinated be pressing against the plastic wrap, when this happens remove it.

Place the jar in a sunny location and water the seedlings every day or two and.

- Cilantro Harvesting Instructions -

Snip a few leaves from each plant gently, taking care not to cut any of the leaves from any one plant.

12. GINGER

Ginger is a favorite of home gardeners from root to harvest. This spicy superfood is known for reducing inflammation and soothing nausea. Raw ginger has also been shown to help relieve muscle pain and lower fasting blood sugar levels in diabetes.

- How to Grow Ginger -

Ginger has a distinct flavor and is found in many stir fry dishes. Purchasing it in local markets can be costly, while growing it can be simple and rewarding. Ginger prefers a humid climate, so misting on a regular basis is important, as is well-drained soil and partial sunshine.

Purchase a piece of ginger from the grocery store and place it in a tub of compost, making sure the freshest-looking buds face up.

Place the container in an environment of indirect sunshine and wait for new growth to sprout. Keep the soil wet at all times so it doesn't dry out (but never waterlogged).

- How to Harvest Ginger -

Remove the whole plant from the soil, break off what you need, and replant the ginger using the same method as before. Ginger makes it extremely simple for us.

13. MINT

In addiiton to giving a great taste to your mojitos, the peppermint oil present in the mint leaves is a recognized alternative medicine remedy for irritable bowel syndorm. Pure peppermint essential oil should not be consumed though.

- How to Grow Mint -

Begin by buying seeds or starter plants, as well as a big, deep pot with a diameter of about 10 inches. Mint can sprawl. Place the seeds or founder in the jar after filling it with potting soil.

Place the jar in a brightly lit area and water it periodically to prevent the soil from drying out.

- How to Harvest Mint -

Well, guess: snip the needed leaves from each plant. Gently.

14. ROSEMARY

The needle-like leaves are the best companion of many juicy dishes, but Carnosic acid, an antioxidant contained in its heavenly-scented flower, has been shown in animal studies to help reduce weight gain and increase cholesterol levels.

- How to Grow Rosemary -

Begin by sowing seeds or propagating cuttings in a container with drainage holes in the rim, containing soil made from a mixture of two parts potting soil to one-part coarse sand works well.

For every 5 inches of pot, add one teaspoon of lime (the agricultural type, not the fruit!) This will aid in the alkalinization of the soil.

Place the jar in a bright indoor location; rosemary needs at least 6 hours of direct sunlight per day to thrive.

Just water where the top layer of soil is dry to the touch (but be sure not to let the soil dry out completely).

- How to Harvest Rosemary -

Snip a few sprigs from each plant gently.

CHAPTER TWO

The 4 Elements of Houseplanting

The four elements of Nature: Earth, Water, Air and Fire. They compose the symphony Nature is made of. Also for our house plants, I feel, they play a major role to their, and ultimately our, well being.

I translate them in Earth, Water, Temperature and Light. Let's start from the latter.

LIGHT

All of the above elements are essential for plants, but light is the one that provides them with energy and allows the photosynthesis process to happen. Those green leaves work like giant solar panels that align themselves dynamically to absorb as much sun as they need by phototaxis, or movement in response to light. Consider the lighting requirements of your bedroom, home, or space before selecting a house plant that you want to host. According to your available space and windows position you can narrow down your options.

Light is what plants eat! Solar energy is harvested and converted into chemical energy. They convert sunlight into sugar, which they then "destroy" to rise, flower, and flourish. Plants die sooner or later because they are fully deprived of light. The amount of sugar, starch, or complex carbohydrates they have manufactured and processed in their tissues determines how long they will last without illumination. They must metabolize stored food before the shelves run out if they are unable to produce food. Plants starve to death in the absence of light. Houseplants were brought to us from their natural environments, where they had evolved and adapted to local environmental conditions over millions of years. Houseplants that are native to the shady rainforest floor, for example, grow in low light environments. Bear in mind, though, that even in shady natural environments, plants aren't completely in the shade. The sky also provides them with a large amount of ambient light (aka skylight: blue light that radiates from the sky). Plants that are native to the bright sun of the desert, on the other hand, need as much light as your home can offer. The most important environmental criteria to remember when preparing for growth with any houseplant are the strength and length of illumination, as well as the plant's distance from the light source. Human-designed homes are dark in comparison to plant-designed homes, such as a brightly lit greenhouse. When we carry a companion plant into our homes, we must be aware of the amount of light it requires and for how long it requires it. Keep in mind that your plants will need to acclimate to their new environment when you put them in the right sun. Over the course of a few weeks, gradually acclimate a newly acquired plant to full light. Give it two hours a day for four days, four hours a day for four days, six hours a day for four days, and so on. When the plant has acclimated to eight hours of full bright sun every day, it will be able to bear full sun all day without burning.

- Light attributes in your home -

The first step would be to determine which window faces which way. What window offers you the best view of the sunrise when you're getting your coffee in the morning? A window that has an easterly orientation. Keep in mind that when you face the east window, south is on your right and north is on your left. You have the West by your side. The second thing you'll need to find out is how far your plant can be from the window. When the plant's leaves are 2 feet away from the sun, it would only absorb one-fourth of the light it would if it were right next to the window. The inverse square law describes this effect, and you can use this basic mathematical formula to help your plants get the light they need. Who knew there would be math involved, right? All you want to do is grow a plant! But it's just not that difficult. A tape measure and a calculator are what you'll require.

The strength of light decreases as the square of the distance from the source of light, according to this theorem. So, if the plant is 2 feet out, 2 squared (2*2) = 4, and the plant only receives one-fourth of the available sun. For example, four feet away equals one-sixteenth the light (4*4 = 16), and so on. If you can see, the more away your plant is from a source of light, the less energy it gets. By the way, the same law applies to artificial illumination.

High Light. Full Sun All Day, South-facing Window

The brightest potential light for a houseplant is the brilliant, strong sunshine on a cloudless summer day at noon as it pours from a south window. Consider a houseplant on the south windowsill, resting in its pot. The plant has been exposed to direct sunshine this morning and will continue to do so in the afternoon. The light's strength and length are at their peak. The number of hours of light in a south window varies from summer to winter, depending on how long the days are, but it is still bright, direct, and full sun. Under these conditions, a barrel cactus or agave thrives, while an African violet will perish. In reality, most good houseplants will struggle in the direct, unfiltered light of a south window, but those that need a lot of light will thrive.

High Light. Bright Indirect Light, South-facing Window

Consider covering a south window with a sheer, lacy, or gauzy white curtain. Your plant is now getting very bright, yet filtered light, thanks to the curtain that hangs between it and the glass. In this way the plant is no longer in direct sunlight, yet it is also in a high-light environment. Your choice of curtains will further alter the light intensity. The brighter the light, the more "see through" the curtain, and the darker the curtain, the less light.

Medium Light. Full Sun Half A Day, East and West Facing Windows

An east or west curtain, in comparison to the illumination of a south window, cannot achieve a full day of sunlight. They just have a half-day of bright, clear sunlight; the majority of the day is filled with skylight. Plants in east or west windows get a medium amount of light. In the morning, as the sun is rising and the air is cold, an east window would have a high light intensity. All afternoon, the east windows will be dimly lit. In an east window with cool morning sunshine, most houseplants will thrive. When the sun is setting and the air temperature is hot, a west window would have a high light intensity all afternoon. During the morning, the west windows will have low light intensity. Many heat-loving plants, such as cacti and succulents, will thrive in a west window because they enjoy the sunny afternoons.

Medium Light. Dappled Light

Venetian blinds on a window facing south, east, or west that receives absolute, clear, intense sunlight imitate the dappled light that a plant receives from an overhanging tree. When the sun moves through the horizon, a plant on the sill of a window with Venetian blinds experiences contrasting bands of strong hot sun and cold shadow that pass across the plants. Through opening or closing the blinds to make the light and shade bars narrow or wide, you can monitor how much light the plant receives. As a result, the plant receives half clear, strong sun and half cooling shadow, which move around the plant's surface.

Medium-Dark. Light that has been filtered

Filtered light is created by drawing a sheer or gauzy curtain over a south-, east-, or west-facing window.

Low light, with north-facing windows that are shaded all day.

North-facing windows are seldom exposed to direct sunlight. The ambient blue light from the sky is the only source of light for them. In the winter, when the sun is low in the sky and the days are small, north windows have a low light setting. The majority of houseplants would not thrive in a north window; however, the cast-iron plant and a few others do. If you only have access to a north window, you may want to try growing houseplants in artificial light rather than natural light.

Low Light. Ambient Light All Day from Sky lights In The Ceiling

Some residences have skylights installed in the ceilings of various rooms. They put the sky's ambient blue light into your home every day. Plants that thrive in low-light environments can thrive in the light produced by these skylights. Skylights, on the other hand, cause a sliver of clear, bright sunlight to pass through your room from morning to night. If your plant is in a spot where it will be illuminated by a bright, concentrated patch of sunlight, you will need to switch it out of that spot for a couple of hours per day. With the changing seasons, the direction that patch of sunlight follows over your space varies. Make sure the plant doesn't get sunburned by following the direction of the patch.

Artificial Light

You can forget about your windows and skylights and cultivate houseplants (almost) everywhere with artificial light. Today, there is a huge selection of light fixtures that are ideal for houseplants. They vary in complexity from plain desk lamps with plant containers at the base to multi-stacked shelf structures with lighting above each shelf. With these light systems in operation, you can brighten up every dark corner with houseplants. Choose a light source that emits the proper wavelengths of light for your plant, regardless of the device you use. Plants use various wavelengths of light for different applications, and different types of lamps emit different wavelengths of light. If all you want is good foliage growth, you'll need blue and red light, but if you want your plant to bloom, you'll need red and far red light. To assess the light output of a lamp, look at the box it comes with. Standard cool-white daylight fluorescent tubes produce blue and red light, making them ideal for vegetative growth. They do an excellent job for foliage trees. Grow lamps, which are special fluorescent bulbs intended to stimulate plant growth and flowering, are costly but designed to emit the correct level of light (blue, red, and far red). They often reduce the amount of heat generated by incandescent, high-intensity discharge, high-pressure sodium, and metal halide bulbs. LED lamps are both low-heat and energy-efficient artificial light sources. The size of the plant you intend to grow is a final factor. Because of the inverse square theorem, tall plants, such as palms, other trees, and big shrubs, are difficult to get near enough to your light source for the light to do any good. Concentrate on low-growing plants that can be placed next to the bulbs if you want to cultivate houseplants under artificial lights in your home. African violets, lady's slippers, and moth orchids are among the best options for this.

WATER

Water is another essential factor of plant survival; even desert-loving plants, such as cacti and many succulents, need watering at some point; however, we seldom consider that a plant requires water to thrive. Water is needed for many physiological functions in the life of a plant, including growth and metabolism. Water in nature is a mean of transportation, think rivers.

Many of nature's inorganic elements can be transformed by plants into carbohydrates, which are then converted into organic compounds, which we eat. This is accomplished by the use of water as a vehicle and improvements in cell osmotic pressure.

Any watering method or device should aim to keep the soil moist but not soggy or dry. Overwatering causes root rot, which is the leading cause of death for all plants in containers, whether indoors or outdoors. This happens because the vast majority of people believe that taking care of a plant means just watering it once a day. This truth, more than any other, demonstrates that proper watering is not as simple as it seems, and that most people overwater. When it comes to water requirements, not all plants are made the same. Some plants, such as bananas, need a lot of water, while many cacti, for example, would perish quickly if they were sprayed as much as a banana plant. Never use cold water straight from the faucet to water your houseplants. These tropical beauties are shocked by the cold water. Using calm, tepid (not cold, not hot) water at all times will bring the best results. Fill a pitcher or jug halfway of water and leave it to warm up to room temperature overnight. Another option is to turn on the hot water for long enough to marginally warm the cool water and remove the chill.

WHEN SHOULD WE WATER?

A quick finger test will help you figure out when it's time to water your plants. The dry potting medium should be at room temperature on the pot's surface. Stick your finger down into the potting medium, and the tip of your finger will soon feel cool, damp dirt. Measure the thickness of the dry medium at the pot's surface with your finger. If you don't trust your finger or don't want to get it dirty, there are a variety of instruments available to decide whether a plant has to be sprayed. Most of the probes are battery-operated and to be inserted into the potting media. These have either a scale with an indicator needle or a digital readout that can help you assess the thickness of the dry potting medium. Small porous clay artefacts (some formed like little earthworms) that you inject into the potting medium are another kind of way to gauge the soil. When wet, these pebbles become black, and when dry, they become light. The plant's label will give you precise instructions about how much water each specific plant needs. You should use:

- Plenty of water - When the surface of the potting medium is dry to a depth of 0.5 inch, water plants that need a lot of water.
- Water in a Moderate Level - When the top of the potting medium is dry to a depth of 1 inch, water plants that prefer mild water.
- Water Levels are Low - When the top of the potting medium is dry to a depth of 2 inches, water plants that prefer low water.

Although watering your plants when the potting mix appears to be dry may sound like a smart idea, it isn't necessarily the best option. Overwatering is a common error, and you can check to see whether the plant really needs water right now or whether it can wait. Here are few tried and true techniques for determining whether or not your plant needs watering.

- The Finger Test: Nothing beats the finger for portability and accessibility. Put your forefinger up to the first knuckle in the dirt. Water the soil if it is dry. This technique is suitable for medium-sized potted plants. Small pots can be disturbed by sticking your finger in them, and big pots are frequently too deep. The chopstick test is a simplified variant of the finger test that operates in big bowls. Insert a wooden chopstick into the dirt and pull it out. There is no need to use water if the chopstick is moist and dirt is stuck to it. It's time to water it until it's clean and dry.

- The Pick-Up Test: For small and medium-sized bins, this approach works well. Simply take the container off the ground. Since dry soil weights less than wet soil, a light container indicates that a plant is thirsty. My friend has a smart indoor gardener who stores her houseplant on a postage metre. When it gets lighter, she waters.

- The Eye Test: If you pay attention, you'll quickly know the signs that each of your plants needs to be watered. Plants that are well-watered seem to be in the right place. Water is turgid in their cells, and they stand firm. When plants are thirsty, they develop a grey sheen on their leaves and look slightly limp. Catching a plant at this point, before it wilts, will save it from irreversible damage from underwatering.Using several methods when watering your houseplants whether you're new to it or uncertain.

Here are a few indicators that it's time to water:

• Soil Probe: this probe will pull soil out of the ground, allowing you to determine how dry the soil is under the surface.

• Moisture metre: this device measures how dry soil is on a scale.

• Lifting the Plant: heaviness indicates that the plant has a lot of water, while lightness indicates that the plant is dehydrated.

• Wilting: usually when a plant wilts, it's because it's not having enough water. Lift the plant to determine if it is light or heavy.

• Tipping: If the plant's leaf edges start to brown and feel crispy to the touch, it's time to water it. If the leaf edges are turning brown but the plant is mushy, it has obviously received too much water.

• Yellow Leaves: Yellow leaves may indicate too much or too little water in a plant, but this should be assessed in each individual case.

WATERING FREQUENCY

The frequency at which you can water your plants is determined by their needs, the porousness of your containers, and other factors.

Clay (terracotta) pots that haven't been glazed are brittle. Since water evaporates rapidly through the walls of these pans, they dry out quickly. These pots are used to "breathe" in gardening jargon. Pots made of plastic, glazed ceramic, glass, or metal do not breathe. Since their surfaces are water-resistant, the potting medium remains damp for much longer than it does in unglazed clay containers.

Watering frequency is also influenced by ambient air temperature, humidity, and daylength. The need for water in a houseplant increases as the temperature rises, as well as it explodes into vigorous growth or starts to bloom. Even if the plants are indoors and shielded from temperature fluctuations, you can water houseplants more often on sunny, dry summer days than on cold, wet winter days. Another thing to think of when it comes to watering your houseplants is the potting medium. A general-purpose potting medium is designed to absorb and preserve adequate moisture, to allow free water to drain away adequately, and to provide enough air for healthy root growth. Some potting media, such as African violet mixes, are produced to hold a little more moisture than a regular potting medium. Other potting media, such as cactus mix or orchid bark, are designed to drain well and do not retain much liquid.

PROVIDE DRAINAGE

Never leave a houseplant with the bottom of its container submerged in a puddle of water in its saucer for more than an hour. You've done a decent job if the potting medium is damp (not soaking wet, but bone dry). You should stop watering your plants until you see water pouring out of the drainage holes at the bottom of the pot. You should make the water lay in the saucer whether the pot is propped up on pot feet or pebbles so that the bottom of the pot does not rest in a pool of water. This pool of water could lead to raise humidity levels. Check back after 30 minutes to an hour if your pot isn't propped up on pot feet or pebbles.

Flush the saucer and discard the water if there is any remaining water. Replace the plant in the saucer and you're done until the next time you need to water it.

WATERING CANS

Many houseplants want a small watering can with a very narrow spout. The tall, clunky, 2- or 3-gallon watering can you use in the yard, the one with the 3-inch-wide nozzle with a few hundred holes in it, is a poor watering tool for your houseplants. Leave the clumsy one in the greenhouse and replace it with a dedicated one for your indoor plants. It should be small and compact, with a narrow spout to guide the flow of water. Place the narrow nozzle of your small watering can on the potting medium's surface and spray the water on the medium rather than the vegetation. This is especially critical for African violets, whose leaves would be destroyed if water is dripped on them.

AIR HUMIDITY

The process by which water passes through the body of a plant is called transpiration. The stems accumulate water from the soil, which flows upward through the stem and out through the leaves. Water vaporizes and escapes the leaf into the air through special openings called stomates. The capacity of your plant to lose water via its leaves is an effective and necessary process. Transpiration, like the heart pounding to pump blood to every cell in the body, bathes every cell in a plant's body in nutrients carried by sweat.

A plant's leaves lose water more slowly while the humidity is high. A plant's leaves lose water easily when the humidity level is low. Two other factors often affect this process. The first is the availability of water. The plant would be able to get the water it needs by mining the soil with its roots if the potting medium is properly moist. In comparison, if you forget to water the plant and the medium becomes dry, the plant will quickly die. The temperature of the ambient air is the second factor to consider. When the air temperature rises, humidity decreases; as the air temperature falls, humidity rises. If you put your plant too close to a hot air register or another source of heat, the water in the leaves would quickly evaporate. Depending on whether your air is dry or humid, you can spray your indoor plants once a week.

HEAT

Temperature is another usually underappreciated aspect of plant health. A plant either falls into the "warm" category or in the "cool" one. As in most the things in life, also plant categorization according to the temperature they can live in, has no such clear black or white. Plants like Christmas or Thanksgiving cacti (Schlumbergera sp.), for example, require a certain amount of cold and darkness to bloom year after year, while others can't survive lower temperatures because it could lead to a stop in their photosynthesis.

Most seedlings, in order to develop properly, need a lot of warmth. This is because warmth, moisture, and humidity will cause a seed to crack and eventually allow a seedling to emerge, after which it will seek out light.

The general practice to follow is that when the plant is growing it requires to be relatively warm, and when it's sleeping - usually during the Winter period - it likes a slightly cooler temperature. No houseplant though likes very cold conditions and even the briefest exposure to frost can be deadly.

When raised inside, many houseplants can’t cope with temperatures below 50 Fahrenheit (10 degrees Celcius). When placed outdoor in summer, it is generally suggested to take your houseplants in before the first frost, so that they don’t suffer from cold damage.

Many blooming houseplants, those which are most commonly growth, such as Begonias, Bromeliads, Tillandsias and many others are best grown in medium room temperatures.

These kinds of houseplants tend to like it a little bit of warm during summer (averagely 65 to 75 Fahrenheit for most begonias) and then like a cool rest during winter (in the 60 F range).

I would say that as. general rule of (green) thumb you shouldn't expose your plants to any extreme temperature.A few might even tolerate it, but that doesn't necesseraly mean that they are having a good time.

The effects of too much heat:

- Wilting leaves and flowers
- Crispy and dry leaves edges
- Thirsty appearance
- It's winter but they are growing spindly

The effects of too little heat:

- Leaves curl and fall off
- The plant is visibly dying (watch out for cold zones between curtain and window)
- The soil is constantly damp with mold or fungus
- Very little growth.

Knowing the regular temperature regime (daytime high and nighttime low) that a particular houseplant requires to thrive under your treatment is critical to its success. The said, plants, on the other hand, are somewhat forgiving, and can adapt to day or night temperatures within a ten-degree Fahrenheit range. Each houseplant's plant label determines the ideal temperature range for that plant, both during the day and at night. Plants cannot produce food (sugar) by photosynthesis while the sun is not shining, so night temperatures are important for houseplants. The plant must burn some of the food it produced during the day in order to sustain metabolism and growth at night. The process of plants metabolising food is known as respiration. Respiration is the polar opposite of photosynthesis and is highly dependent on temperature. If the temperature rises, so does the rate of metabolism. As the nighttime temperature rises, a plant can hit a point where it has eaten up all of the food it produced during the day. If the plant burns out all of its backup food stock at much higher temperatures, it is bound to be dead in no time. This is the reason why when you bring those irresistibly adorable little miniature roses in 4-inch pots home from the supermarket, they die within a few weeks. Our homes' humid overnight temperatures ruin them. If you plant them outside in the garden where the nights are cold, they are not only content but also lovely. They are not houseplants, as they're virtually all temperate zone plants.

The first thing you must know of your plant in which temperature category it falls:

- High Temperature - Plants that thrive in extreme heat prefer temperatures of 75 to 85 degrees Fahrenheit during the day and 65 to 75 degrees Fahrenheit at night.

- Moderate Temperature - Plants that prefer warm temperatures thrive in temperatures between 70 and 80 degrees Fahrenheit during the day and 60 to 70 degrees Fahrenheit at night.

- Low Temperature - Low-temperature plants can withstand a daytime temperature range of 65 to 75°F and a nighttime temperature range of 55 to 65°F.

HEARTH

Because of the multitude of available choices, picking up soil at a garden center can be a daunting task. Yet, it's crucial to pick the right soil. Garden soils and potting mixes are not interchangeable and cannot be used in the same way. Any soil can be modified and tailored to produce a plant-perfect mix.

- **CLAY**

In comparison to other kinds of soil, clay soil is thick and moist. It retains a lot of water and compacts quickly. While clay soil can be difficult to garden in due to its density and moisture levels, there are many plants that can thrive in it. In clay, many ornamental grasses and prairie flowers thrive.

Organic matter, such as fertilizer, leaf mold, and well-rotted manure, can help strengthen clay soil. The easiest way to amend clay soil is to include organic matter: It improves drainage and aeration, moderates soil temperature, and provides pore space, all of which are important for plant development.

- **SAND**

Gritty sand is nutrient-poor and drains easily. Sand isn't a perfect potting soil on its own, on the other hand, it is often used as a soil amendment to increase texture and drainage in other forms of soil. Natural ingredients, including clay earth, may be used to boost it.

• SILT

Crumbly silt retains minerals and moisture, but it compacts like mud. Silt particles are a happy medium for tiny sand particles and massive clay particles. This kind of soil is often regarded as a hybrid of clay and sand, combining some of the benefits and drawbacks of both.

• CACTI AND SUCCULENT MIX

Cacti and succulents need well-draining soil to grow, which is why many producers create a blend especially for them. To provide the drainage that these plants need, this form of soil contains an equal mix of sand, perlite, and potting soil. You can buy this kind of soil, but you can also make your own by mixing one-third horticultural sand, one-third cactus compost, and one-third grit (pumice, perlite, or porous gravel) together.

• PREMIUM MIX

Plain potting soil may be a decent fit for plants, but it will need to be supplemented with a few corrections to help them survive. For a premium blend of ingredients, apply perlite, composted waste, vermiculite, and peat moss to potting soil. A premium soil mix can also be purchased in supermarkets. When growing edibles, be sure to look for organic potting soil. Non-chemical fertilizers are used in organic blends, which is safer for the earth than the plants.

• ALL-PURPOSE MIX

For most plants, a mixture of peat moss, vermiculite, and composted bark works well. Many all-purpose soil mixes provide time-release fertilizers, which provide nutrients to plants for a longer period of time. Although most all-purpose blends are not organic, a few firms do produce a substance that is less chemically enhanced.

POTTING MIXES

What you get when you buy a package of "potting soil" from the nearest garden center isn't really soil. It's a man-made combination of materials intended to satisfy the needs of container plants, and it typically doesn't contain any natural soil. Since garden soil, or plain old dirt to others, becomes increasingly thick and airless over time, it does not encourage good container plant growth. In the greenhouse, where it profits from the behaviors of worms, insects, fungi, and bacteria, garden soil is completely sufficient. However, a pot is not the same as a greenhouse, and every plant in a pot has unique requirements that cannot be fulfilled solely by ordinary garden soil. Roots in a pot, like roots in the greenhouse, need oxygen to survive. But for orchids, most plants' roots are not green and cannot provide food by photosynthesis. Roots must metabolize the sugar produced by the leaves in order to remain alive and expand. In plants, this mechanism is known as respiration, and it involves the burning of sugar to release energy while still consuming oxygen. It is painful and life-threatening to your houseplant when the air (oxygen) in the medium around the root system of your houseplant is drained, whether due to long-term absorption by water or close density of the medium.

Inorganic mineral products such as perlite and vermiculite, which produce air spaces in the medium, are combined with sharp horticultural sand to facilitate drainage in artificial "potting soil." To hold and maintain moisture, it also includes organic content such as bark fines. In a pot, such a mixture never becomes as thick and airless as garden soil. The organic fraction of the medium, on the other hand, would appear to retain more moisture than is ideal for the plant when it breaks down and decomposes with time. After that, it's time to repot with new medium.

As I said, technically, potting soil isn't soil at all. It is a mixture or combination of various materials that feed the plant, such as sphagnum moss, perlite, bark, compost, vermiculite, or coir.

The soil-less combination is chosen because soil attracts spores and bacteria that can cause the plant's death. The soil's various components also ensure improved drainage, increased nutrients, and even fertilizers in the mix. Potting soil is costly, and it's best used for indoor and outdoor plants in pots, planters, and containers.

Potting mixes were created at a time when there seemed to be an endless supply of sphagnum peat moss available as a primary ingredient. Unfortunately, those days are gone, and much of the sphagnum peat moss deposits have been depleted. Instead of peat moss, more environmentally conscious potting soil manufacturers are now using bark fines from tree farm timber logging or coconut coir from coconut plantations as the moisture-retaining organic part of their mixes. Potting soil that is organic. Apart from the primary ingredients mentioned above, most healthy general-purpose organic potting soils often contain nutrients derived from organic fertilizers (manures, compost, worm castings), mycorrhizal fungi spores, and CFUs (colony-forming units) of beneficial bacteria. These mixes' organic fertilizers release nutrients slowly and do not destroy plant roots. Non-organic potting soils are not advised because they often use dried, water-soluble fertilizers. For starters, non-organic processed fertilizers are more concentrated than organic fertilizers, putting the plants at risk of root burn. For another, non-organic commercially prepared potting soils follow a one-size-fits-all approach, and they're designed for annuals like petunias, tomatoes, and the like, not houseplants. For plants with specific requirements, commercially prepared potting media is readily available. While the majority of these are not organic, you can easily produce your own organic blend. Unique media, which you can purchase or make yourself, is beneficial to three types of houseplants.

• Succulents and cactus 1 part sharp horticultural sand, 1 part perlite, and 1 part organic potting medium for general use This well-drained blend is ideal for all types of cactus and succulents.

• African Violets. For truly good African violet growth, commercially prepared African violet potting media is often too thick and holds too much moisture. You can make your own by mixing 1 part industrial African violet blend with 1 part organic potting medium for general use.

• Orchids. The majority of orchids grown as houseplants are potted in chunks of straight Douglas fir bark or other types of tree bark that lack bark fines or other moisture-holding components. Many orchids thrive in bark with just a little help from poor fertilizers. If you put them in potting dirt, they will die. There are three types of orchid bark: coarse, mild, and fine. For most adult orchids, coarse and medium bark would suffice. For seedlings, miniatures, and other small plants, use fine orchid bark. The root zone of the bark media is exceptionally well drained, with wide pore spaces and plenty of oxygen.

Cymbidiums and lady's slippers, on the other hand, do not grow well in straight orchid bark. To make a well-drained medium for these semi-terrestrial orchids, combine 1 part fine orchid bark with 1 part general-purpose organic potting medium.

Difference Between Potting Soil and Gardening Soil

The difference between regular gardening soil and potting soil is important. Using planting soil in your pots and planters will prevent the plant from reaching its full potential.

The plants would be deprived of vital nutrients, water drainage, and growing conditions if they were grown in gardening soil. Potting soil is loaded with all of the nutrients a plant need.

It also aids in the drainage and distribution of water uniformly for the plant to absorb, as opposed to gardening soil that clumps together and absorbs water, destroying delicate plants. The tendency of potting soil to drain well is the primary reason it is used by most indoor plants.

Gardening soil also includes a variety of insects and fungi that are harmful to plants. Since the potting 'soil' is devoid of soil, it does not harbor these dreadful pests.

Potting soil, on the other hand, is expensive, making a big dumping ground in your garden uneconomical. They can only be used for container plants so drainage in containers and pots is more difficult. Plants in your greenhouse do not have this problem and can thrive in planting soil.

Components of Potting Soil

Potting soil, as previously said, is a combination of various materials. The proportions of the components decide how nutritious the plant can be.

• Peat Moss

This is the most commonly used ingredient in any potting soil. Peat moss is the decayed remains of sphagnum moss that has died in bogs and has been there for thousands of years, and it comes from peat bogs.

The partly decomposed material is excellent for either retaining additional moisture in plants or breaking up clumps for improved drainage. It's both low-cost and lightweight. That is why peat moss, also known as sphagnum moss, is a popular ingredient in potting soil.

• Pine Bark

Pine bark by itself isn't really beneficial to plants since it lacks nutrients; but, when mixed with peat moss, it may be transformative, as it can provide more air space for the plants while still assisting with water and fertilizer retention.

It is obtained from paper mills and incorporated into the potting mix.

• Perlite

The potting soil often contains tiny white shards, which are an essential factor. It's known as perlite, because it's made of hot volcanic glass. It is added into the potting soil to keep it from being too dense and heavy, as well as to allow water to drain more easily.

• Vermiculite

Vermiculite is a volcanic mineral that serves the same function as perlite, namely, to increase the number of air spaces in the sand and strengthen circulation.

Vermiculite, on the other hand, differs from perlite in that it helps retain a little moisture as well as fertilizer, meaning that the fertilizer and other nutrients are not flushed away but remain in close proximity to the roots for a longer period of time.

• Coir Fiber

Coir Fiber is a by-product of the coconut industry that serves the same function as peat moss, but at a lower cost and with less environmental impact.

• Limestone

Pulverized limestone is often applied to the mix, mostly to neutralize the peat moss' pH level. It's also well priced and convenient to locate.

• Sand

Sand is excellent for irrigation too and is widely used in cactus mixes.

The Different Types of Potting Soils

• All Purpose Potting Soil

This potting soil is ideal for most container-grown indoor and outdoor plants. It's a generic blend of ingredients that isn't based on any particular plant family. If you don't know which potting soil to buy and don't know where to start, all-purpose potting soil is your best bet.

• Organic Potting Soil

Natural, plant, and animal-based ingredients, such as worm castings, food compost, manure, bones, and decayed plant and animal matter, are used to make organic blend. The organic matter is extraordinarily fertile.

• Seed Starting Mix

This is a very fine potting soil mixture that creates perfect germinating conditions. It is deficient in nutrients, causing the plant's roots to branch out in search of food and nutrients, allowing it to rise and spread rapidly.

- Orchid Potting Soil

Orchids need good air circulation over all else, as well as well-drained soil to keep the roots from being too damp. This blend was created specially to aid the growth of certain delicate orchids.

- Cacti and Citrus Potting Soil

Cacti and citrus plants need strong drainage as well, so sand is applied to these particular mixtures to aid drainage.

- Moisture Control Potting Soil

These mixes have moisture-controlling pellets that prevent the soil from drying out completely, allowing the plant to absorb as much moisture as it needs.

- Outdoor Potting Mix

These are commercialized for outdoor container plants, and have the same soil environment as these plants would have had if they were emerging in the wild. They typically have a higher concentration of fertilizer and moisture-retaining pellets. They are usable also indoors if you have it already, but it's usually better to rely on one of the others.

The contents of commercial fertilizer packages are often defined as "plant food." This is a misunderstanding. Fertilizer provides mineral nutrients like nitrogen, phosphorus, and potassium that plants need for growth, but the sugar that plants produce from sunlight and carbon dioxide is what they consume. You are really feeding your plants while you breathe on them. They take in carbon dioxide from your breath, combine it with solar energy through photosynthesis, and use it to make sugar. The sugar provides them with the energy they need to produce new leaves, roots, branches, and flowers as they metabolize it. Plants require 12 vital mineral nutrients in addition to sunshine, carbon dioxide, and water. Animal droppings, dying animals, and dead plant material are all sources of these nutrients in nature. Houseplants must gain nutrients from their more confined environment: if you use an organic potting medium that includes organic fertilizer and compost, the plant will receive the nutrients it requires. The vast majority of houseplants are unconcerned with nutrients, but if the potting medium is devoid of fertilizer, you may need to supplement with organic fertilizer. After the plant has matured, you will need to fertilizer it again. To assess a plant's fertilizer requirements, look at its portrait. On the front of a fertilizer box are three numbers (e.g., 6-12-4 or 10-10-10), which represent the percentages of nitrogen (N), phosphorus (P), and potassium (K), in that order. Since plants need comparatively large amounts of these three vital nutrients compared to the other nine, they are referred to as primary or macronutrients. The first number, nitrogen, is essential for vegetative development. Nitrogen is needed for the growth of new leaves, roots, stems, and other parts of a plant. Since high nitrogen encourages the lush growth of green leaves, any houseplant grown for its attractive foliage rather than flowers needs a high-nitrogen fertilizer. Flowering and solid roots require phosphorus (the middle number). Phosphorus is needed for the initiation, growth, and maintenance of flowers in plants. This is why phosphorus levels in fertilizers for flowering bulbs are so high. Any flowering houseplant that is cultivated primarily for its attractive flowers rather than its foliage needs a phosphorus-rich fertilizer. Potassium (the last number) helps plants grow strong stems and protects them from stress. If your plant is getting enough potassium, it will be able to tolerate extremes (too much or too little) of important environmental variables including sun, temperature, and water.

Calcium, magnesium, and Sulphur are secondary important mineral nutrients. They are not needed in the same amounts as macronutrients, but they are still essential for healthy plants. Boron, copper, iron, manganese, molybdenum, and zinc are six micronutrients that are needed in minute amounts. To remain healthy, plants need all 12 of the mineral nutrients mentioned above. They also use the carbon, hydrogen, and oxygen that they receive from carbon dioxide and water in order to produce sugar. All 12 of the necessary mineral nutrients needed by your houseplant should be supplied by a fine, high-quality organic potting soil containing organic fertilizer.

The Choice of the Fertilizer

Soil can supply essential nutrients to a plant, but since most of our plants are kept in closed environments, they don't get nearly as much resource exchange as they would if they were outside. That implies that soil would need to be renewed on a regular basis, which is usually accomplished by fertilizing a plant. The worst mistake anyone can make is giving a plant too much fertilizer, or not enough in some situations. More fertilizer can appear to help a plant grow, but it may also inhibit particular types of nutrient uptake, such as phosphorus, which is necessary for protein synthesis, cell division, and development. Plants don't need to be fertilized too much during the non-growing season, so it's necessary to understand how they want to be fertilized and why it's usually handled with a very dilute medium.

Some might wonder what kind of indoor plant fertilizer is best. I suggest that you go to a garden center and look for a fertilizer labelled "indoor vine." Since you'll need less fertilizer indoors than outdoors, make sure you use the rate recommended for indoor plants. If you're buying fertilizer for blooming plants, look for one labelled with the form of plant (orchids, for example), but if you're not sure, you can use fertilizer for houseplants instead.

Ferns, succulents, and sansevierias can all get plenty of sunlight and just the right amount of water, according to any decent plant owner. This simple care will keep your plants alive, but if you want them to flourish, fertilizer might be necessary. While fertilizer is often referred to as "plant food," this isn't exactly accurate. Photosynthesis provides food for plants, but they also include micronutrients and macronutrients for enzyme production, water regulation, and plant defense.

Instead, fertilizer includes an assortment of micronutrients as well as the three primary macronutrients that plants require: nitrogen, phosphorous, and potassium (abbreviated as NPK on product labels). Nitrogen aids leaf and stem growth, phosphorus aids root development and flowering, and potassium aids disease resistance.

The balance of these three components is represented by numbers on all fertilizer labels. For example, a 10-10-10 fertilizer contains ten percent of each. Different fertilizers have different concentrations, making it difficult to determine which is right for the plants. From orchids to cacti, we asked experts to decipher the labels and break down the best formulas.

What is it Good For?

Fertilizer is used to absorb vital nutrients that the soil can lose over time. To keep those levels up and your plant healthy, you'll need to bring nutrients back into the soil through fertilizer. Since orchids are epiphytes, or plants that grow on other plants and depend on them for help but not food, you'll want to apply nutrients less often if you have a plant like an orchid that uses peat moss or bark chips instead of soil. Fertilizer is not needed for newly potted plants or low-light plants.

How to Choose?

The brand name of a fertilizer isn't relevant when shopping for one. It's the N-P-K ratio that matters. The main macronutrients your plant requires are nitrogen, phosphorus, and potassium. N-P-K would be more in the lines of 15-30-15. Higher ratio fertilizers are more dense than lower ratio fertilizers. Micronutrients can be used in your fertilizer, rendering it a full fertilizer. Calcium, magnesium, boron, iron, zinc, Sulphur, nickel, manganese, copper, and molybdenum are some of these elements. Each micronutrient has a specific function in the enzymatic, cellular, and developmental processes of plants.

Best All-purpose Fertilizers

Chemical fertilizers are produced with a near-perfect volume of both macro and micronutrient and are made from ground minerals.

They're much more concentrated and, in most cases, less expensive than organic varieties.

Organic fertilizers are the mildest of all since they are made entirely of fresh materials. Organic fertilizers are naturally stinky since they have a rotting organism. Be sure the organism is worth the stench in your house and that it is supplying the plant with the right amount of nutrients. You can do it yourself or buy it ready-made if you're not feeling adventurous. Organic fertilizer is more expensive than other varieties, but it is a chemical-free choice.

Organic and chemical fertilizers also provide nitrates, potassium ions, and phosphates to plants in different forms. Organic is not inherently better than conventional, but if you choose to live a healthy, ecological lifestyle, organic is the way to go. It's a delicate balancing act of personal taste, both yours and your plants'.

There are several different types of fertilizers to choose from, which is one of the reasons why deciding which one is better for indoor plants can be so difficult. Here are a few examples of various types:

• Liquid Fertilizers

Water is used to dilute liquid fertilizers, which are then sprayed with a watering can. You can fertilizer every time you water or every other time, depending on the instructions on the package. The frequency depends on the type of plant, as some, especially those with huge, dramatic blooms, may require more regular feeding. Often do your homework on plant specifications and find out what they need in terms of nutrition. Liquid fertilizer gives you a consistent supply of nutrients that you can monitor. It's simple to stop feeding while the plant is inactive, such as during the winter, or to resume feeding when the plant is producing new growth. However, the downside is that you must try to do so every time.

Liquid fertilizers can added to the irrigation system. Some formulations or plant feeds may be used once or twice a month. One of the best things about liquid fertilizer is that you have a lot of control over how much is applied. During periods of stagnation, you can stop fertilizing and double-check that no fertilizer has already been released into the field.

On the other hand, the disadvantage is that you would have to add nitrogen to the water at the appropriate time, which is easier said than done.

- Granular Fertilizers

By hand, pure fertilizer pellets can be blended into the potting soil. While they are most widely found in outdoor gardens, they can also be used in indoor containers, but doing so is more difficult. When the pot is watered, granular fertilizer spills all of the nutrients at once, making it difficult to monitor how many the plants get at once. While this form of fertilizer is cheap, it is not ideal for feeding houseplants.

The soil and granular fertilizers are used together. When you first put a plant in the pot, it does exceptionally well and spreads the granules in the container. Granules are difficult to use on indoor plants because they consume all of their nutrients at once as the plant is drained, and it's difficult to determine how much the plants need. Ignore the warnings on the packet to avoid overfeeding or underfeeding the plant.

- Slow-Release Fertilizers

Many gardeners and experienced growers have rapidly adopted these brands as favorites for both indoor and outdoor plants. Slow-release fertilizers have time-release shells that allow nutrients to slowly leach into the soil. Since the coatings on the individual pellets are varying thicknesses which melt at different speeds, the fertilizer release is phased across time. The duration of a single application will range from four to nine months. The biggest disadvantage is the increased cost of slow-release fertilizer, but this is offset by the fact that it lasts too long.

Slow-release fertilizers come in a variety of forms, including spikes, nuts, and pellets. They have a time-release covering that aids in the slow penetration of nutrients into the soil. Since there is less area to cover and you don't have to worry of nutrient delivery too much for this kind of fertilizer, it works better in tiny containers.

One disadvantage of slow-release fertilizers is that it is impossible to predict how easily the nutrients can spread. The time-release shield can, in theory, always keep things back a little so you never really learn.

POTTING YOUR PLANT

The majority of people want to replace their houseplant's original pot with a more appealing one. Overall, your companion plant should blend into your decor and be housed in a container that matches your home, and those small, thin-walled plastic pots from the nursery just don't cut it.

CONTAINERS

The pots that we are going to use for our houseplants are going to be smaller than most of those that we could use for example in a container garden in out backyard.

These smaller pots are measured by diameter in inches. A 4-inch pot, for example, would have a diameter of around 4 inches, with manufacturers that vary greatly in their pots measures: some 4-inch pots in fact are bigger, with a 4.75 inches of diameter, while others are smaller, measuring 3.5 inches across.

Larger pots are usually represented in terms of height. A 1-gallon pot has an average diameter of 8 inches and a height of 7 inches. A 2-gallon pot is approximately 10 8 inches in diameter, a 3-gallon pot is approximately 11 - 9.5 inches in diameter, and a 5-gallon pot is approximately 14 - 10 inches in diameter.

The depth and shape of the pot can make a big difference. Tall narrow pots will be better for plants that like moist conditions and shallow wide pots are better for plants that like dry conditions.

You can find inexpensive, thin-walled plastic pots used by nurseries for plant processing in hundreds of different sizes. When you buy a houseplant, it typically comes in a 4-inch or 1-gallon container. Palm trees, citrus trees, and shrubs such as hibiscus can all be grown in a 2-gallon or 5-gallon pot. In any case, the plant would most likely come in a cheap black or green plastic jar with a thin wall. A houseplant container may be anything that houses an amount of potting medium and has a drainage hole.

If you wish to cultivate your plant in an old boot, for fun, design or just experiment, you could do so: all you have to do is drill a hole in the boot to ensure proper drainage. Wood, tin cans, glass pots, terracotta, fine porcelain, bronze, fiberglass, and plastic can all be used as houseplant containers. I myself have created an exposition of the strangest containers I could turn into pot in section of my living room. Just make sure there is at least one drainage hole in anything you use. If there isn't one, you'll have to either drill one or use the jar as a cachepot (a decorative shell for the "real" pot). Drilling holes in ceramic containers is easy with a half-inch carbide bit and a 3/4-horsepower electric drill but be careful since your expensive porcelain or hand-thrown ceramic jar can be easily damaged during the drilling process. It is usually easier, and safer, if you hire a specialist to drill the holes instead of doing it yourself. On a hard ceramic board, it takes a lot of effort to press down on the drill, and the noise is utterly deafening. If you still want to go fo the DIY, make sure to cover your ears, eyes, and hands by wearing earplugs, masks, and gloves.

As per the shapes of the pots, a wide-bodied pot with a narrow neck at the top is one of the most beautiful jar shapes. These are lovely pots, but they're probably the worst option you could choose for a houseplant. The issue is that you have to take your plant out of its pot on a regular basis. If the neck is shorter than the body, you'll have to either cut the roots or split the container to get the plant out. Pots with straight sides or ones that flare out wide with a collar that is wider than the body are far safer options. These shapes make it simple to cut the plant without causing damage to the plant or the container.

If you can't bear the look of your plant's hideous pot but it's not ready to be up-potted into the beautiful shiny new porcelain, brass, or hand-thrown tub you bought to match your decor, you can make it a cachepot. The cachepot is simply a beautiful pot that hides the ugly pot. Just plop the ugly pot into your pretty pot and call it a day before your plant is ready to be up-potted. If your cachepot is too heavy for your plant even though it's about to go up, up-pot it to a larger but equally cheap and hideous pot when it's ready and place it back in the decorative cachepot until your plant is big enough to support the amount of soil in your cachepot. If the bottom of your lovely cachepot doesn't have a drainage hole, you'll need to fill it with 1 to 2 inches of clean pebbles. Place the ugly pot on top of the pebbles so that the ugly pot's bottom is never submerged in water. Carefully water your plant, never allowing the water from the unsightly pot to climb above the pebbles in the bottom of your cachepot. If you inadvertently bring in too much water, make sure to pump it out so your plant doesn't get waterlogged.

Another method for watering is to carefully take the plant out of the cachepot and place it in the kitchen sink or tub, where you can water it, drain it, and then return it to the cachepot.

REPLANTING

Examine your plant when you first get it to see how it will benefit from being transferred to a larger container (up-potting). Pull the plant out of its container and examine the root ball. If you treat the plant gently, it will not be harmed. If there are just a few roots visible on the sides of the root ball and the potting medium begins to fall apart when poked with the finger, push the plant back into its tub and wait a year or two before up-potting. You should up-pot the plant into a larger jar if the root ball is surrounded by a safe network of white roots that are tightly holding the mass of potting medium in a compact ball as you remove it from its cheap plastic tub.

Another thing to consider is how quickly plants evolve. Some houseplants grow slowly by birth, while others grow quickly, but both may need to be re-potted at some stage. Use a tape measure to estimate the diameter of the old original pot when you're sure your plant is ready for a new, larger pot. When it's time to shift your plant to a bigger pot, it's important to know the size of the jar.

The new pot can be about 2 or 4 inches bigger than the old one. What is the reason for this? Since a small plant with a small root system is simply incapable of extracting moisture from a large amount of soil, the potting medium becomes too damp for too long, causing the roots to rot. You must gradually increase the size of a plant's pot until it reaches the size you expect it to remain in it for a long time. The new pot should be 2 inches greater in diameter for a slow-growing tomato. The new pot should be 4 inches bigger for a fast-growing tomato. To put it another way, if you're up-potting a slow-growing plant in a 4-inch pot, you can switch it to a 6-inch pot. This will give you 1 inch of fresh potting medium wrapped around the root ball on both sides. Place a fast-growing plant in an 8-inch pot when you up-pot it from a 4-inch pot. This will add you 2 inches of fresh potting medium around the root ball on both sides. A fast-growing plant will easily fill 2 inches of new potting medium with healthy roots, but a slow-growing plant will not be able to do so.

Keep in mind that certain houseplants, even when fully grown, will still be minute. An African violet comes to mind as a plant that will never grow big enough to be considered a tree. And when fully grown, it will remain small and will comfortably fit in a 4-inch pot. In comparison, a rubber tree in a 4-inch pot will easily outgrow the container and will need to be up-potted to a larger container. Since the rubber tree is a woodland giant in the wild, if you give it a big enough pot, it will comfortably hit the ceiling in your house.

RE-POTTING

You don't want to switch your houseplant into a bigger pot once it has achieved the ideal size for your space (i.e., you don't want it to grow any larger than it is now). You re-pot a plant and bring it back into the same jar, or a similar-size container, to limit (or maintain) its size. Remove the plant from its jar and inspect the roots. You'll most likely see a twisted mess of firm roots with no potting medium visible. Cut off 1 inch of the root ball on both sides and around the bottom with a clean, sterile, sharp knife. Put the plant back in its container and fill the bottom of the pot with 1 inch of fresh potting medium, then fill the sides of the pot with 1 inch of fresh potting medium. Your plant will need to be re-potted in two to three years, when you'll simply repeat the process.

PLANTS PROPAGATION

Once you have your plant army set and ready in your house, it's just normal to wanting, at least your favorite ones, to make babies. This process in houseplants' terms is called propagation. Now, in nature plants take care of everything on their own. In the case of our green buddies housemates we may need to help them in order to recreate our beautiful plant to fill that bright corner of our living room or to give it as a present to a friend.

Asexual propagation techniques such as division, cuttings, and layering are tried and tested ways to produce exact copies of your parent plant. Each plant has a propagation method(s) that can be used for that specific plant. However, you should be conscious that certain cultivars are covered by patents. You are allowed to lawfully cultivate as many patented plants as you choose, but only for personal use. It's against the law for you to sell them. These plants may only be sold by the patent holder or licensee.

Sterilize Your Tools

Cutting or wounding the plant with a knife or pruners is a popular technique for propagation. But the first thing you must make sure of before you start cutting your vine is to make sure the tool you're using is clean, sharp, and sterile. A vast amount of viral and bacterial diseases can infect plants, and the viruses and bacteria that cause them are normally transmitted from plant to plant through the knives and pruners we use, so let's sterilize our equipment. Say you use a pruner on a virus-infected plant and then use the same pruner on a healthy plant without sterilizing it between the two operations, there is a high chance forthe healthy plant to become infected. Cymbidium mosaic virus and ringspot virus, for example, are found in orchid collections all over the world. Orchid growers use a blow torch to sterilize their pruners, to eliminate any virus spores attached to the blades. African violet growers disinfect their equipment by soaking it in rubbing alcohol. Another option is to soak your equipment in a 10% bleach solution for a few minutes (1 part household bleach to 9 parts water). Be careful not to exaggerate with the bleach, as it corrodes the equipment, but a correct proportion kills bacteria very effectively. Another option is to use single-edge razor blades meant to be trashed after use use or reused by wrapping them in aluminum foil and boiling them in water for 20 minutes, which is though the most time consuming option.

DIVISIONS

The simplest approach for producing exact copies of your houseplants is simple division. Simply divide the plant into two or more parts. However, you must reduce water loss if you break pieces off your vine, otherwise your divisions will desiccate and die. Remove one-third to one-half of the leaves from each division to achieve this. Break the leaves in half or cut them off at the bottom of the branches. Rhizomes, tubers, stolon, pups, and keikis are the five forms of divisions.

• Rhizomes - A rhizome is a specialized horizontal underground stem that sends out new shoots at frequent intervals in certain houseplants (many orchids, ferns, snake plant, cast-iron plant, etc.). Break this rhizome into two or three parts with a clean, sterilized, sharp knife or pruners, making sure each piece has its own roots, stems, and leaves. Pull the parent plant apart gently as you go to disentangle the seeds.

• Tubers - Underground tubers can be found in calla lily, caladium, and gloxinia. During the dormant time of the plant, cut the tuber into two or three parts with a clean, sterilized, sharp knife.

• Stolon - Spider plant and creeping saxifrage, for example, have unique aboveground stems called runners or stolon that produce plantlets (just like a strawberry plant). Break this runner into two or three pieces with a clean, sterilized, sharp knife or pruners, making sure each piece has its own roots, stems, and leaves.

• Pups - Around the base of the old mother plant, other houseplants (all bromeliads, many succulents, some cacti, a few palms) grow new shoots, or pups. These pups may be separated from their mother plant and placed in their own pots until they have enough roots. Using a clean, sterilized, sharp knife or pruners, separate the pup from the parent plant. Make sure you have a good number of roots.

• Keikis - On their old flowering stems, moth orchids often produce a keiki (Hawaiian for "child"). While still attached to the old inflorescence, these tiny plants grow leaves and roots. With a clean, sterilized, sharp knife or pruners, remove them from the mother plant when they appear large enough to live on their own. Be certain to collect all of the stems.

All divisions should be potted in the same potting medium as the initial vine. Place a glass jar or plastic bag over each division until it is back in productive development to keep humidity up and reduce water loss. Every day, for around an hour, open or close this cover to let air in. Maintain the divisions in a warm, low-light setting, water sparingly until they've developed a strong root system in their new position and are aggressively producing new leaves. Remove the cover and acclimate them to their permanent position in the suitable light and temperature conditions for that specific plant until they are completely grown.

CUTTINGS

Another simple technique for propagating houseplants is to cut parts of stems or leaves. Most houseplants have stems that will sprout roots if the circumstances are correct (palms are an exception and will die if the tops are cut off). Just a few plants have the ability to produce new plants from their leaves. Each plant has a specific propagation method(s) and stem tip cuttings, stem cuttings, and leaf cuttings are the three styles of cuttings.

- Stem Tip Cuttings

Remove the top 6 to 8 inches of the stem tips to make a simple stem tip cutting. Cut just below a node (the point where a leaf is or was connected to the stem), this is where the new root structure will emerge. Remember to always sterilize and clean (and sharpen) your knife or pruners. All but the top two leaves of these cuttings should be removed, and the remaining leaves should be cut in half to limit water loss and avoid desiccation and death. Dip the bottom end in rooting hormones, then place the cuttings in wet sand. Place the cuttings in a glass of water if you like. Many, but not all, stems may develop roots. The roots can be seen through the bottle. When the leaves resume active growth pot them up.

- Stem Cuttings

Break off the leafy top of a plant if it has grown too tall and handle it like a stem tip clipping. Your pot would be left with nothing but a bare stick or cane growing out of it. The bare cane can sprout a new leafy tip, but if you want your plant to be much shorter, cut 6- to 8-inch-long pieces from it and root them according to the instructions below. A new top will emerge from the stump you've left behind. Do not attempt this with a palm because it will die. Cut the topless cane off at the new height you want your original plant to become with a clean, sterilized, sharp knife or pruners. Mark the bottom of the cane you just lopped off (the opposite end from the leaves) with a marker so you know which is the bottom (toward the ground) and which is the top (toward the leaves). If the stem segment is long enough, cut it into 6- to 8-inch sections, mark the bottom of each segment once more. The plant can tell which way is up and which way is down. Roots will only grow from the bottom end, and shoots will only grow from the top end, so make sure you don't plant it top down and bottom up.

Allow three days for the parts to air dry. Plant them in wet sand, and new roots and shoots may emerge from the stems. If they've developed a strong root system, pot them in the same potting medium as the original plant.

• Leaf Cuttings

Rooting the leaves of a few plants is a simple way to disperse them. Several leaf cuttings may be placed in a single pot or tub filled with damp sand or a 50/50 mixture of perlite and vermiculite. Put a glass jar or plastic bag over each pot to keep humidity up and minimize water loss. Every day, for around an hour, open or close this cover to let air in. Keep the leaf cuttings warm and out of direct sunlight. The formation of roots can take several weeks. If you gently pull on a leaf cutting, you'll be able to see if it's rooted or not. They'll have developed new little plantlets in a few months. You can now pot them up in individual pots using the same potting medium as you used with the original plant.

Leaf cuttings are particularly useful for propagating four types of plants:

• Snake Plant - Using a clean, sterilized, sharp knife or pruners, cut a leaf from the parent plant. Label the bottom of the vine, the end nearest to the potting soil, with a pen. Break the leaf into 4-inch-long sections, making a mark on the bottom of each one. The leaf remembers which way is up and which way is down, and if you plant a piece of leaf upside down, it will simply die. Allow your leaf fragments to air dry for a day or two before planting them in moist sand or a 50/50 blend of perlite and vermiculite.

• African Violets, Streptocarpus, Gloxinia - Fill a pot halfway with perlite and vermiculite and water before water seeps into the drainage holes. With a 1- to 2-inch stub of the petiole (leaf stalk) attached, cut middle-sized leaves from African violets (or their gesneriad relatives, streptocarpus and gloxinia). Use a sharp knife or pruners that have been cleaned and sterilized. Place the cut end of the petiole in rooting hormone, then into the moist perlite and vermiculite blend you've already packed. Several leaf cuttings may be placed in a single jar. In 2 to 4 weeks, the leaves will have rooted and will begin to produce baby plantlets. Pot the baby plantlets when their leaves are around 1 inch long.

- Begonias - Begonias cultivated for their leaves and/or flowers may be propagated in the same way as African violets are, with the exception that the petiole stub must be narrower, 0.5 to 1 inch long.

- Jade Plant and Other Succulents - Most succulents root well from their leaves. Using a clean, sterilized, sharp knife or pruners, remove the leaves and dip the cut ends in rooting hormone. Allow 3 days for air drying. Fill a pot with a 50/50 blend of perlite and vermiculite and spray until the drainage holes are completely dry. Place the dried leaves on top of the potting mix. Place them on top of the medium rather than sticking them into it. Succulents can rot if placed in a plastic bag or under a glass container. Water the potting mix around the leaves, but not on the leaves, to keep it moist. Use a pencil-thin spout on a very shallow watering can. Keep the leaves as dry as possible. In around a month, you'll see tiny roots and a baby plantlet sprouting from the leaf's end.

All cuttings should be planted in the same potting medium as the original plant. Place a glass jar or plastic bag over each cutting until it is back in active growth to keep humidity up and reduce water loss. Every day, for around an hour, open or close the cover to let air in. Keep the cuttings warm and out of direct sunlight. Water sparingly until they've developed a strong root system in their new position and are actively producing new leaves.

LAYERING

Layering is a method for growing roots on a stem that is already attached to the mother plant. Plants can be layered in two ways: air layering (time-consuming, tricky, and challenging), and simple layering (fast and convenient).

Simple Layering

Plants with long, versatile stems, such as pothos and arrowhead vine, are particularly easy to reproduce by layering. Spider plants and creeping saxifrage, for example, have lightweight specialized stems called stolon that can be easily handled with this technique. Everything you have to do now is choose a jar for your freshly propagated plant to flourish in and fill it with the right potting medium for it. Set the container close enough to your mother plant that you can pick up a healthy stem or stolon and place it on the top of the container after moistening the potting medium with water and letting it drain.

• Stolon - You can find small plantlets at the nodes of a stolon. Place one of these small plantlets in the center of your container by adjusting the angle of your pot and stolon. Pin the stolon to the potting medium with a U-shaped staple or a strip of wire, with the tiny roots pressed deep into the dirt. The moist potting medium will activate the roots, causing them to rise. Cut the stolon and break the bond between the little plant and the mother plant after a few weeks, when the little plant is well rooted and vigorously producing new leaves.

• Vines - Switch the location of your pot to insert the fourth leaf from the tip of the stem in the middle of your jar to propagate a plant. Pothos is an example of a plant you can use this method with. One or two fat little roots will normally protrude from the node (the point where the leaf connects to the stem) on the opposite side of the stem from the leaf. Push these tiny roots into the ground. Pin the stem to the potting medium with a U-shaped staple or a slice of wire with the leaf pointed up. Remove the leaf with a clean, sterilized knife or pruners and throw it away. On the node away from the mother plant, you now have a stretch of stem with three leaves. The mother plant's stem is already attached to it. The moist medium will activate the roots at the node pinned to the potting medium, causing them to expand.

The dormant bud at the node where the cut leaf was connected to the stem should grow out into a new stem and be well established after a few weeks. In order to sever the connection between the little plantlet and the mother plant, cut the stem between them at this point. You now have a new little plant with two developing stems: the three-leaf stem tip and the new stem that sprouted from the node.

Air Layering

This is the most time-consuming and complex method of houseplant propagation, but it is a great tool for plants like rubber tree and fiddle-leaf fig that are difficult to root using other techniques. You're attempting to allow a stem produce roots when it's already connected to the mother plant, similar to basic layering. However, unlike vines or stolon, these plants have stiff, non-flexible roots, making it impossible to fold one down to tie it to a potting medium container without crushing it. A solution is to bring the potting medium up to the plant.

If you need to go for this method, here are 12 steps to an efficient air layering plant propagation:

• Choose a point 8 to 12 inches down from the tip of a good young stem and cut one-third of the way through the stem at an upward angle just below a node with a clean, sterilized, sharp knife (the place where a leaf was attached to the stem). Cut the stem no more than one-third of the way in, then hold it above the wound to prevent it from breaking off.

• Remove a leaf or two if they are in your way.

• When a rubber tree or fiddle-leaf fig is wounded, it bleeds a milky white sap that dries to rubber. And use a damp cloth to wipe away the sap.

• Put a toothpick horizontally into the cut to prop it up.

• Apply rooting hormones to the cut and cover it with a handful of moistened, stringy sphagnum moss.

• Cover the moss ball in a cylinder of two layers of plastic when keeping it in place.

• Use electrical tape to seal the top and bottom of the package but leave the top loose enough to apply water to the inside.

• In a few days, pour enough water inside to keep the sphagnum moss moist.

• You'll see new roots growing within the plastic in a month or two, but roots will take up to eight months to grow, so be careful.

• Strip the plastic covering when the new roots are around 2 inches deep and cut the parent plant's stem just below the new little root ball. The sphagnum moss in the root ball should not be removed.

• Pot up your new plant.

• Place it somewhere warm and shady until it adjusts to its new existence away from the original plant.

SEED

Any houseplants can be easily grown from seed. Growing a decent-sized woody plant like a citrus tree takes a long time (years), but it is much easier for herbaceous perennials like geraniums. Furthermore, seeds are the products of sexual reproduction, and seedling is one distinct entity from its mother plant, much like your own infant. You must reproduce the plants asexually by division, cuttings, or layering if you wish to produce an exact clone of them.

Many houseplant seeds come with specific instructions written on the box or in their catalogues about the proper sowing medium, sowing depth, soil temperature, watering, and light regime each type of seed requires in order to germinate successfully.

CHAPTER THREE

Grooming your Housplants

To stay healthy and good-looking, houseplants need to be groomed on a regular basis. Regular care not only improves the appearance of your plants, but it also helps to keep pests and pathogens at bay.

Without daily grooming, houseplants get filthy or tangled. If you don't keep an eye on it, your indoor gardens will lose a lot of their appeal, so cleaning and grooming the houseplants is an essential part of their upkeep. Why would you want to have an indoor houseplants garden if they don't look beautiful?

Dusting and Cleaning Houseplant Leaves

Dust on a plant's leaves put at risk their ability to survive. In order to grow, leaves need to be able to breathe. Dust can clog the breathing pores (stomata) in the leaves, limiting the amount of light that can reach the growth-activating cells.

Many houseplants are stored and cultivated for their lovely leaves alone and the elegance of your indoor garden is diminished if the leaves get dusty or damaged. Cleaning the plants' leaves then is a fundamental - but often undervalued - habit to develop. The method for doing so varies depending on the leaf and its texture.

- If they have a smooth surface you can wash the leaves with a wet cloth. Rubber plants (Ficus elastica) and Swiss cheese plants (Monstera deliciosa) are two examples of plants with leaves that can be dusted this way.

• Plants with a number of smooth-surfaced, but smaller leaves can be flipped over and immersed in clean water.

• When the smooth-surfaced leaves are big use a soft cloth to gently dust them, before brushing them with water.

• If you have fuzzy or hairy leaves, try brushing them with a gentle and soft brush.

Clean, soft water that is not chalky is ideal for washing leaves. If you live I a place where only "hard" water is available, you can use rainwater or boiling tap water instead. Milk, vinegar, or beer may also be used, but the leaves will not be as shiny. Another alternative is using olive oil, although it retains pollen, which can eventually damage the leaves. Leaf-cleaning items are also available on the market, but generally I'd suggest to turn to the above methods.

Removing Leaves and Stems

A houseplant's appearance may be ruined by dead or misshaped leaves. Damaged leaves and misplaced plant shoots should be removed. You can use sharp scissors to hack overzealous stems down to just above a leave-point as they wreck the plant's form. Simply hack out the dead leaves, being careful not to leave little snags that would die back. If the dead leaves are at the top of the shoot, the only way to get rid of them is to cut the stem down to its base with sharp scissors.

Dead flowers on houseplants may be picked off separately and tossed onto a compost heap. Azaleas bloom for several weeks and contain a large number of flowers. Pick off the first ones as they die to make room for the new ones to rise. This is referred to as deadheading.

For instance, as you are deadheading a cyclamen you should take off each dead flower along with the stem. It will snap off where you want it to if you just give it a pull. If you just cut the flower, the stem can eventually decompose, causing other flowers and stems to decompose as well. It also seems to be unattractive. Remove the flowers and stems from the plant and place them in the compost heap; do not leave them at the base of the plant.

Deadheading Flowers

The same process can be done with flowers. Remove any dead flower heads as soon as you see them with clean, sharp pruners or scissors. Dying flowers on a plant are not only unsightly, but they are also likely to rot, leaving them vulnerable to grey mould attack.

The growing seeds are removed by deadheading too. Breeding seeds drain the plant's resources until the seeds are harvested and used. By cutting the flowers as they die, you can make your plant bloom stronger and allows the plant to focus on producing more buds.

Fruit trees should not have their flowers chopped off or they would not produce fruit. Since certain house plants, such as hoyas and orchids, can bloom again on the same flower stem, it's a smart idea to get to know your plant and learn when and how to cut off the flowers.

Shaping or Training Your Houseplant

Climbing plants are plants that sometimes may be a bit more challenging to manage. They need support and preparation in order to look their best. To keep stems from sprawling and getting tangled, we should train and assist the growing vines and this is where splint canes and acrylic wire frames come in handy. Pink jasmine (Jasminum polyanthum), on the other hand, looks better when sliced and embraced in a circle or heart shape.

The first step is to put a pliable cane into the pot when the stems are around 12 in. (30 cm) long. To avoid destroying the plant roots, position it near the sides of the container. The next step will be curling the plant shoots around the support; this will give your indoor garden area a neat new form as well as added charm and appeal.

Small trellises may be used to prevent climbing plants to get mould. Place them near the pot's side to avoid damaging the plant's roots, and thread the longer shoots through the trellis. Until the plant hasn't matured on its own you'll have to train her guiding the stray strands the way you want them to grow.

Pinching Plants

The term "pinching" refers to the act of cutting a plant's rising top. When plants get so tall and leggy, cutting the top of the plant reduces the plant's height while still allowing it to grow bushier. Pinching also aids in shape maintenance and in controlling the growth of some of the more robust plants.

Cutting back vining plants falls into the pinching as well. To pinch a branch, merely remove a small portion of the tip with your fingertips or pruning shears. When a plant is pinched, new shots form quickly to fill in the gaps. Although pinching isn't something you can do every day, take a look at the plant from time to time to see whether pinching would change the shape and appearance.

When it comes to training and pruning container houseplants, many gardeners are intimidated. To keep an attractive jar, some grooming is needed at some stage. While light trimming can be achieved at any time of year, it is better to prune house plants while they are actively growing, which is typically in the spring and summer months.

If you pay attention to your plants needs, it's simple to build gorgeous indoor gardens. Your garden will flourish wonderfully for years to come if you keep them under a caring eye.

THE BENEFITS OF PRUNING YOUR HOUSEPLANTS

1. Gets Rid of Damaged Leaves and Stems

This is critical since infected leaves and stems will potentially deplete the plant's energy supply. You're taking some of the job off your plant's plate by extracting those dead pieces, helping it to focus its attention on healthy leaves and new growth!

If any of your leaves are infected with bacteria or fungi, it's safe to remove them so that the infection doesn't spread to the rest of the plant. It's all a matter of proper hygiene!

2. Keeps Your Plant from Getting Too Big

Some plants, such as indoor trees and climbing plants, may grow violently toward the sun, causing them to become too big or tall for their environment. Pruning the plants will save this from happening and will give them a more compact appearance.

3. Give Your Plant Balance

Depending on where the plant gets its light, it can expand sideways toward the nearest window, resulting in a lopsided or unbalanced plant. (And I believe you don't want your plant to fall over!)

To avoid this, rotate the plant on a daily basis so that it grows symmetrically. Plants can also get out of balance, and pruning can help prevent lopsided development.

4. Decreases Crowded Areas

To stay safe, plant leaves need airflow and space. If the plant 's space becomes overcrowded, the leaves can rub against each other, causing damage, or restricting airflow, and putting the plant at risk for diseases such as mildew. Pruning can help to thin out populated areas.

HOW TO PRUNE YOUR HOUSEPLANTS

While light trimming can be achieved at any time of the year, it's better to prune house plants while they are actively growing, which is typically in the spring and summer months.

Before you prune your houseplants, make sure to do the following:

1. Choose Your Timing Wisely

Most plants benefit from pruning during the spring, when there is plenty of light to encourage regeneration and new growth. Thisi is why pruning is suggested in the spring or early summer seasons. Dull tools or scissors will crush the stems and harm your plant, so you'll want to invest in a good pair of pruning shears. Put your gloves on for safety and you're ready.

Lay down an old sheet or a drop cloth before you start, particularly if you're working with a big plant or tree. Some plants secrete a sticky sap that can stain your floors and irritate your hands. (It's a good idea to do a fast Google search for your specific plant to get a sense of what to expect.) Pruning a pothos is easy but pruning a huge Ficus tree would definitely necessitate gloves and a drop cloth.

Then, since germs on your tools will infect your plant, you'll want to clean and disinfect them beforehand. Before you start pruning, run your shears through the dishwasher or vigorously wash and dry them with soap and water.

2. Planning Your Cuts

Consider how you want your plant to look when you're through before you begin. Since you can't erase a break, it's best to prepare ahead of time where you want to make your cuts.

A nice little trick here is to use a little Post-it Note or colored tape to mark the leaves or branches you wish to trim. You'll be able to schedule the cuts and make corrections before cutting it.

3. Don't Go Overboard

Some plants will withstand severe pruning, while others may need a more gradual approach. In general, the hardier the plant species, the more you can cut without it going into shock.

Snake plants, philodendrons, spider plants, pothos, and other similar plants usually don't mind if you cut many of their leaves. More susceptible plants, like Ficus trees, on the other hand, could go into a shock if you cut too many leaves at once. If you have any doubts, study your plant first, and don't cut more than 10% of the leaves at once.

Remove any leaves or branches that have been damaged. Get rid of any leaves or branches that have noticeable spotting, dryness, or discoloration first. This way you'll free up your plant's resources for it to focus on healthier growth.

4. Reduce Crowding

Intend to clean out any overcrowded areas in your plant. Mark any branches that are touching, dense clumps of leaves (that aren't characteristic or attractive for your species) or leaves and branches that are obstructing another's development.

This will increase ventilation, reduce the chance of fungal development, allow for unrestricted growth, and simply improve the appearance of your plant.

5. Shape Your Plant

You should now start worrying about aesthetics if the tree can afford to lose a little more after you've decided which leaves and branches need to go to improve the tree's health.

Consider the general form you want your plant to take. You will want to cut any leaves or branches that stick out in odd directions from your vine. Consider where you'll need to cut to get your plant down to a reasonable size if it's just getting too high.

It's now time to prune!

HOW TO MAKE YOUR CUTS

Cut the sections you've labelled with your sharp, clean tool. Make sure the cuts are clean and that the branches aren't smashed. If this occurs, you may need to sharpen your tool or change your cutting motion.

To get rid of the leaves remove any sick or disabled parts of the plant and dispose of them in the trash. If you compost them, you run the risk of infecting other plants.

Watch out for those healthy part that shows stable growth, as you may want to keep them for propagation. Or, this might be when you cut them properly for your plant to propragate.

You might want to keep for if you're eliminating it.

After Pruning Your Houseplants

If your plant is in good shape, it should bounce back from the pruning and start growing again in a few weeks. Don't panic if the plant looks a bit droopy for a few days. It might be experiencing some shock, but it will recover quickly.

Tip: Fertilize your plant on a regular basis to help it heal and begin to thrive again.

CREATING YOUR PERSONAL PLANT SANCTUARY

An indoor garden can be a refuge from the outside world and a source of immense pleasure for many people. Introducing such plants into your household, whether you live in a tiny apartment or a big house, will start to increase your health and overall satisfaction. Plants can help with loneliness and sadness, as well as improving the mood and providing a calming living environment. Caring for a living thing gives us a meaning and is satisfying, particularly when you see that living being bloom and flourish.

Spending some time studying which plants are ideally fit for each room and what kind of ecosystem, can help you build your ideal green haven. Here I give you a few suggestions derived from my experience:

- ***Choose the Right Plants for The Optimal Night's Sleep***

While plants emit oxygen during the day, it's important to note that when photosynthesis ceases at night, most plants turn gears and emit carbon dioxide. This is the reason why it is not suggested to keep houseplants in your bedroom. Anyhow, plants like orchids, succulents, snake plants, and bromeliads, do the same, just with an opposite timing, and emit oxygen at night, making them ideal bedroom plants (alos helping in enjoying a better sleep).

- ***Avoid Too Much Sun***

Most indoor plants dislike direct midday sunlight, so keep this in mind when choosing plants for your house. Leaf fire, spotting, or abrupt leaf-fall are both visible warning signals to keep an eye out for. Don't be alarmed; most plants can be safely saved. It's usually a case of not overwatering them or allowing the soil to dry out a little if it's too wet. Check for a cold draught above your vine, as this will cause the leaves to curl and gradually fall off. Organic fertilizers are a fantastic way to bring your plants back to life.

- ***Jazz It Up***

Plants are a fatherly inexpensive way toliven-up even the most boring rooms. If you're not satisfied of your salon, plants are a simple and beautiful way to dress up the living room. Succulents on windowsills, bright macramé hangers from curtain rods, or something large and bold like the beautiful fiddle leaf fig, are all options available to refresh our spaces. You can also have some fun with the pots by displaying your plants in lovely ceramic and copper containers. Plants can embellish the most modest room and plant ownership does not have to be costly: just take a cutting from a friend's plant or purchase a cutting from your nearest plant shop and propagate your plant from the ground up.

- ***Some Plants Like It Hot***

When it comes to plant styling, knowing the plants that are suitable for which rooms is crucial: for example, the bathroom is ideal for air plants and kokedama (Japanese hanging moss balls), as the extra moisture from your everyday shower makes such plants thrive. If you have a sunroom or a room that gets a lot of sun, fill it with ferns, palms, succulents, and cacti, as they thrive in the heat.

HOUSEPLANT STYLING TIPS FOR YOUR SPACE

Bringing indoor plants into your home or workplace is a perfect way to add color and texture to your surroundings. It can be difficult to know how to dress your plants. All should appear deliberate and put-together, but it should also appear natural and in keeping with the rest of your house. Years of experience taught me twelve essential tips to style your houseplants into your home environment, twelve simple plant design solutions to recreate and to freshen up your space.

1. Add a focal point by combining interesting or engaging containers with living plants. Group three plants together in various sized pots with contrasting colors. To break up the visual look, make one of the three larger. In groups of three, everything looks better.

2. Embrace simplicity. Use a clean, transparent, or decorative vase to hold a plain yet large plant frond. Try a monstera leaf or a related cutting from a larger plant with its lovely form and cutouts. Take a cutting from your pothos or other green plant and put it in an interesting container if you don't have much room. The emphasis is on the pairing's interesting shapes, texture, and simplicity.

3. Add a terrarium to your world. Terraniums are magical. A terrarium in your home is not just a focal point, but it is also a world within a world, and it is simple to create and preserve. Terrariums come in a variety of styles, from basic to intricate, and they need minimal maintenance. Moisture or mist is released from the vegetation and plants in a terrarium, which is captured on the glass walls and trickles down into the soil, effectively watering itself. Together with your houseplants terrariums are a great way to relieve tension and fear while also adding some style to your home or workplace.

4. Add style with patterns and interesting materials. Containers and pots are an excellent complement to the style toolbox. Consider terrazzo, leather, or a ceramic glaze or geometric pattern. Stripes or color-block patterns may be added. Consider how the structure and the texture of the pot or container can contribute to your "plants room" with any variation you make.

5. Embrace your ceiling. That's right. Don't be afraid to use hanging plants in your home decor. Hanging planters may be used to view a beautiful plant next to a window or glass door. Plants that flourish in natural light thrive in indirect light, so use your home or office windows as a habitat for your houseplant. Keep an eye on their water requirements, since a colder, clearer climate would necessitate more frequent watering. There are a big variety of hanging planters available. I personally use planters with straps made of braided fabric, with pots made of resin, which makes them more durable.

6. Create an urban jungle. Plants that emerge in a vine-like manner look fantastic in hanging planters and on a table or bench. To bring the jungle into your home - to give the impression of a dense wall of green - choose bushy, full, sturdy plants. A couple of them should have a trendy pot for variety. When the plants will have outgrown the room, prune them back, it's simple. A variegated pothos is a hardy plant that grows quickly and needs no maintenance and it's perfect for this. Alternate this Pothos with neon pothoses, with their vivid green hue, will give the green wall a nice pattern of greens.. In this terrazzo pot, place a bright, modern-looking plant, like a Swiss cheese plant (Monstera deliciosa). If you want a more classy yet elegant appearance, a grey ceramic cylinder is perfect.

7. Create a focal point. Create a focal point by grouping pots or containers of the same color. A set of identical colored pots on a shelf, table, or fl oor will bring calm to your room and relax you. Stack many white or cream pots with different plants of varying sizes. You'll see the appeal right away.

8. Pair an indoor plant with another object Create a scene or a pattern, using a sculpture, a drawing, or an image,. Pots and planters can be combined to create a grouping that will attract attention to your room and make it more fun for your visitors. Everything you pick would look great with your plant and pot. Keep in mind the law of threes, and you'll be styling in no time.

9. Embrace plants with sculptural shapes, particularly succulents and air plants that need little attention. Succulents come in a wide range of colors and shapes, each of them is different and physically appealing. The key to growing succulents is to avoid overwatering them, that's pretty much all you have to do, beside looking at them.

10. Make an effort to be interesting. Air plants are one of the most important plant groups to search about. With their unique shapes, sizes, and colors, you can't go wrong by adding a few of these in your space. Air plants are themselves living sculptures that will bring visual appeal to your space, from the symmetrical spiral of the Xerographica to the vibrant Tillandsia Cyanea. A collection of air plants will grow in low light or bright light in a transparent glass terrarium or displayed in one of the geometric air plant hangers on a table group. Taking care of them is as easy as soaking them in water once a week. Other than that, there isn't much more that needs to be done.

11. Add a plant stand. The new range of plant stands available to help showcase a plant in a home or office is one of the most interesting changes to the plant world switch from the outside to the inside. Plant stands, or a grouping of plant stands, may serve as a visual focal point and anchor for a space. They can be placed at a certain height, enabling plants to be shown closer to a seating area or near a piece of furniture, making the plant closer to eye level when seated.

12. Pick unique plants. Houseplants come in a wide range of shapes and sizes, colors, and light requirements, giving you plenty of options for finding something exclusive and fascinating. The splits and holes in the Monstera deliciosa leaves for example make it a common favorite. If you want to embellish your house even more originally, I'd suggest you try a nerve plant, or three "living stones" plants. Or if you want to surprise get yourself a coral cactus.

The argument is that different plant choices, depending on their color, form, and scale, will provide different visual appeal. My suggestion is: be daring! Consider the location of your home and the atmosphere you want to achieve while making your decision. A sansevieria is an excellent alternative if you choose something that is elegant, new, and more contemporary. A common tall anchor plant is needed, and the Fiddle Leaf Ficus or a Bird of Paradise are both excellent choices. Add a few hanging pothos plants or a hoya plant to the mix for an urban jungle effect and see how quickly their shoots rise.

IDENTIFY AND SOLVE COMMON HOUSEPLANT PROBLEMS

It's difficult, if not impossible, to keep your plants alive if you don't know what's wrong with them. A single symptom can mask a variety of problems but diagnosing common houseplant issues is the first step toward bringing them back from the brink of death.

Use this easy pinpoints to figure out which of the most popular houseplant issues is preventing your plant from flourishing, making your life a bit simpler.

The first step to solve whatever problem your houseplants are going through is to watch. Practice a daily attentive observation of your green house mates. Here's a list of what you may notice and what you can do.

1. The Leaves Are Turning Yellow

Overwatering is the most important cause for a plant's leaves turning yellow. Start by giving your plant a haircut and trimming off the yellow bits to solve the problem. It could be as simple as snipping the ends off, or it could be as complex as removing whole leaves. Then, by putting your finger an inch into the dirt, make sure you just water the plant when it requires it. If it's thirsty it's time to drink. Hold off if it's all wet.

It's perfectly safe for older plant leaves to yellow and fall off as part of the natural ageing process. If your plant's leaves, even new growth, are turning yellow, it's likely that it's receiving too much sun. See if this can be solved by transferring it to a location with indirect light.

2. The Leaves Are Turning Brown

While overwatering causes yellowing leaves, underwatering causes browning leaves. Grab a pair of scissors and cut off any brown tips or leaves before watering your plant to keep it strong and sturdy.

3. It's Leaning and Falling Over

It's possible that the plant is leaning or falling over due to nothing more than a lack of support. You can purchase a variety of stakes to provide additional support for your plant, enabling it to grow large and tall.

This is difficult to diagnose since it can be exacerbated by both over- and under-watering. Sticking your finger through the top layers of the soil on a regular basis will tell you the rate and speed it is drying out. You should water again when the top 2 inches (5cm) of soil is dry, as a general rule. You should water the plant right before it begins to display signs of dehydration. The only way to get the watering right is by trial and error, as you understand your plant.

4. The Leaves Are Dropping

If the leaves on your plants unexpectedly drop or turn yellow it's also possible that your home is too cold. Plants can normally withstand temperature fluctuations of 5 to 10 degrees but anything more than that can stress them out. To keep your plants comfortable, keep the temperature between 65°F and 80°F.

5. The Leaves Are Looking Pale

It's more likely that your plant isn't receiving enough sunshine if its leaves are turning pale and losing their green hue. Wen the leaves turn yellow it means that the green chlorophyll pigment is disappearing because the plants aren't getting enough sun. Make sure you understand how much light your plant needs, as each one has unique requirements. Some people excel in bright light, and others thrive in dim light.

6. The Edges of The Leaves Are Turning Brown

It's possible that the temperature in your home is too high if the edges of your plant's leaves are turning brown. The plant's lower leaves can also fall off and wilt as a result of the same problem. Make sure your home's temperature is between 65 and 80 degrees Fahrenheit.

The main causing factors are dry air and/or inadequate irrigation. Over-fertilizing is another cause of leaf burn, which appears as browning tips. When using fertilizer, do follow the package directions and err on the side of caution. It's much easier to over-dilute than to under-dilute!

7. Your Plant Is Growing Extremely Slowly

If your plant's growth has slowed compared to what it was doing before, fungus gnats might be to blame. There's a fair chance there are larvae in the soil if you've seen some buzzing around your farm. After they hatch, they bind to the roots and suck the nutrients from the plant, resulting in sluggish growth and/or yellowing leaves. This problem must be addressed as soon as possible: use hydrogen peroxide & water solution; let the soil dry out; replant the whole plant or change the growing medium and apply insecticide to it. You can also yellow sticky card to attract and trap the gnats.

8. The Leaves Are Spotty

Fungi may be the cause of spotty leaves. Spotting may be caused by a variety of species and manifests as tan, reddish brown, or black spots or lesions that often run together and form larger forms. To save your houseplants, you'll need to remove those leaves as soon as you notice these sings, and this will usually be enough to improve the plant's chances of recovery.

9. Your Plant Is Getting Soft

Root rot, which occurs when your plant is overwatered, can be the cause of your plant's softening and mushy leaves. Although recovering your plant from root rot can be difficult, it is possible. Examin and cut the affected roots to let your plant air dry. Read point n13.

10. Defoliation

Overwatering, underwatering, the need for a bigger pot, inadequate lighting, injury from excessive hot or cold weather, low humidity, mosquitoes, and diseases are all factors which may lead to defolation, when your plant looses all its leaves. Consider each factor, one at a time and observe how the plant reacts.

You will encourage new leaf development by the amount of light available. If increasing the amount of light doesn't work, consider adding fertilizer. Healthy plants rarely drop their leaves unless they are deciduous, which means they drop their leaves and go dormant for a season. Any decent plant store will tell you if the plant goes dormant when you purchase it. Bulb plants and certain Dendrobium orchids are examples of typical indoor plants that turn deciduous. Remember that the majority of indoor flowering plants are evergreen.

11. Leaves Are Curling

his may happen when a plant is exposed to lengthy periods of drought or low humidity. Water as much as possible, then spray the leaves to provide more moisture.

12. Leaves Are Wilting or Burning

This is a telltale indication that the plant is overheating and perhaps being burnt by the sun. Tropical plants, in particular, are readily burned by direct sunlight and should be kept away from windows that magnify the glare. Many indoor plants are especially vulnerable to the afternoon heat.

13. Roots Are Rotting

Root rot causes plants to be unable to retain moisture and nutrients from the soil, causing them to appear dehydrated even though the soil is totally saturated. When it comes to root rot, the only ways to stop it are good drainage and a daily watering schedule.

Remove the plant from the soil and allow the roots a thorough rinse if it can be lifted. Cut the infected roots with a sharp pair of scissors or secateurs. It's also possible that up to half of the foliage would need to be removed. Any fungus present can be killed by dipping the roots in a fungicide solution. To prevent spreading the infection to the newly potted plant, thoroughly rinse the infected pot with disinfectant or diluted bleach.

14. Lopsided Growth

This is more noticeable in some plant species than others, and it is more of an aesthetic concern than one that would damage the plant. The fiddle-leaf fig (Ficus Lyrata) in particular suffer form "lopsiding" if it is not rotated on a daily basis so that both sides of the plant are exposed to the brightest part of the room. As a general rule for every plant, when you water them, try to rotate them a little.

15. Age

In general, if a plant is growing, we tend to believe that it is in perfect shape. There are exceptions, though. If a plant is growing but losing leaves at the same rate as it is growing, it may be pot-bound or nutrient deficient. Or it is just a sign of ageing: as plants age they can lose old leaves. The timing really depends on the plant, but as you see evident signs of age and the plant has not been thriving anymore for a substantial amount of time, it may be time to kiss the plant goodbye. But there is no reason to trash it in the garbage; you can leave it in a wild garden area to decompose, or spread and mulch it on a lawn when it can decompose and contribute to a healthy soil.

When it comes to determining plant health, basic observations are the best place to start. Is it just one leaf that has turned yellow and fallen off, or is the whole plant showing signs of stress?

COMMON PROBLEMS THAT CAN LEAD TO PESTS AND DISEASE

As far as pests go, there are many. The most common include:

- Aphids
- Caterpillars
- Cyclamen mites

- Earwigs
- Eelworms
- Mealybugs
- Red spider mites
- Root mealybugs
- Scale insects
- Thrips
- Whiteflies

But our houseplant unfortunately can also be threatened by diseases, among which: black leg botrytis, powdery mildew, root rot, rust sooty mold, and various viruses. Most of the times those issues are fixed with proper care, removing the ill part, cleaning, changing and renewing the soil. Keep an eye out for signs of your plants distress. There are many options of chemicals product to intervene and save the day if nothing else has helped. You may also use a concentrated insecticide dissolved in clean water and spray the leaves and the stem. This technique is very often used and you can buy ready-to-use liquid chemical sprays in specialized stores where they are readily available. Another option is to use use a systemic insecticide to water the compost, which is going to have access to the plant through its root system. You can find this in stick shape to be inserted in the compost.

Dusting plants is also a good way to get rid of viruses and rodents, but it leaves an unpleasant smell. However, this is a fast and effective way to eliminate pests. Make sure the powder is uniformly distributed and that you do the procedure outdoors to avoid distributing the solvent around or on your furniture. It's really something that you wouldn't like to inhale.

Remember, taking care of plants is not just watering plants. Always pay attention with careful observation. Acting soon is best medicine. Nip those problems in the bud!

MUSHROOMS GROWING IN HOUSEPLANTS SOIL

One of the most annoying things that can happen to our houseplants is a mushroom invasion in their soils. But what causes mushrooms growing?

A fungus causes mushrooms to flourish in houseplants. Mushrooms are the fungus's offspring and the Leucocoprinus birnbaumii is one of the most common mushrooms found in houseplants. The cap of this light yellow mushroom may be balled or blunt, depending on on the level of maturity it reaches.

Normally, polluted soilless mixes introduce spores that allow mushrooms to thrive in houseplant soil. They can, however, be spread in other ways, such as airborne movement or spores brushing off clothing.

Mushrooms most often occur in houseplants during the summer when the temperatures are favorable to their growing. Unlike lawn mushrooms, which prefer cold, damp conditions, houseplant mushrooms prefer wet, moist, and humid conditions.

Getting Rid of Mushrooms in Houseplants

Regrettably, this is not an easy task. It's impossible to get rid of the spores and fungi that cause the mushrooms once the soil is poisoned, but there are a few things you can try:

• Remove the Caps: As soon as possible, remove the caps to eliminate the source of spores that cause mushrooms to grow in houseplant soil. This can also drive mushrooms away from the rest of your houseplants.

• Scrape the Soil: Scraping the top 2 inches (5 cm.) of soil from the houseplants' pot and removing it may aid, but the fungi and mushrooms may reappear.

• Change the Soil: Changing the soil may aid in the removal of mushrooms. One of the issues being that removing all of the soil from a plant's roots (via washing or rinsing) is demanding for the plant and the fungi can still reappear and regrow from the soil left on the houseplant's roots. So clean and rinse the roots carefully.

• Drench the Soil with Fungicide: Drenching the soil of houseplants with fungicide can help in eliminating mushrooms, but they will return if all of the fungus is not destroyed. It is possible you'll have to repeat this procedure several times before the fungus is finally eradicated.

• Change the Conditions: If the air is less hot, the soil is less wet. As the temperature cools off the amount of mushrooms will be reduced. Unfortunately, the conditions that are optimal for mushrooms are also ideal for most houseplants, so altering the temperature repeatedly can damage the houseplant.

Getting rid of mushrooms is difficult, but the piositive thing is that, beside your personal esthetic tastes, most of the times they will not damage your plant. (This is should probably be useless to mention, but: DO NOT think about consuming them!) You may want to try watching them mature on their own. Hey, if you want to be more whimsical, place a few animals or fairy figurines near them and transform your house into a little forest magic garden.

DO'S AND DON'TS: 8 STEPS TO YOUR INDOOR PLANT SUCCESS!

1. Don't Repot Too Quickly!

Do not automatically switch your new indoor plant into a separate pot after purchasing it from a grower. Transplanting too quickly would most likely destroy the plant's delicate roots, and even if the plant does not die as a result of the damaged roots, the stress exerted on the roots will inhibit foliar development. Before you contemplate giving your new houseplant a new home, wait until the roots have had enough time to mature and take hold. Indoor vines like Hoyas and Pothos prefer to be a little rootbound, so a delayed transplant would be particularly beneficial!

2. Avoid Direct Sunlight

When you buy a new plant, particularly one labelled "sun-loving," it's natural to assume that putting it in direct sunlight is the best option. But be cautious! Plants, like most humans, dislike abrupt, dramatic environmental shifts. Unless you know 100% that the plant was residing in direct sunlight prior to your purchase, you can start in a more soft fashion by placing it in indirect, bright sunlight and then gradually introduce it to the direct light in which it would eventually flourish. If you live in a hot climate and choose to keep your new plant outdoors, this is particularly necessary.

3. Don't Water Immediately

Do not think that your newly bought plant is thirsty when you first bring it home. Instead of watering your new plant right away, inspect the soil and roots. Wait until the top of the soil is drying before giving the plant a drink, especially if there is moisture. Overwatering is one of the most common causes of houseplant death. Allowing the plants to dry out between waterings is preferable than watering them too much.

4. Don't Immediately Divide Your Plant

Enable a new indoor plant to acclimate to its new environment and grow more foliage before attempting to divide it from other plant it may have come with. Plants with especially tender roots, such as Maranta and Calathea, will certainly suffer if you break them apart too quickly. Even if you buy a pot with several messy plants you will easily distinguish the plants from one another, just take your time to untangle them with caution to not to rip the roots.

5. Don't Immediately Cluster Your New Plant with Other Plants

Before you put your new plant alongside other plants, make sure it's free of pests and disease when you get it home. While most trustworthy growers work hard to keep their plants safe and clean, some plants can still get polluted or infested.

You should be particularly cautious if you purchase your plant from an unlicensed vendor whose facilities have not been inspected. Anytime you purchase a new herb, leave it isolated for a few days and inspect frequently the leaves and soil. If you see something suspicious, spray the plant with horticultural oil and neem oil alternately. You can easily add your new plant to the rest of your collection after you've taken these precautionary steps.

6. Don't Use Leaf Shine Products

Leaf shine products may temporarily improve the appearance of your new plant's leaves, but the additives will eventually damage the plant by clogging the stomata and inhibiting the plant's ability to breathe. Instead, easily clean the leaves with warm water mixed with herbal soap to produce lustrous results. You can also get the same result by mixing neem oil with water.

Wiping the surface of your new houseplant's leaves clean removes old fertilizer and water residue, allowing your new plant to swap gases and experience photosynthesis regularly.

7. Look Before You Fertilize

Do not fertilize your plant right away if it isn't looking healthy when it first arrives! Since your plant was probably already fertilized by the grower, feeding it further would most likely harm or destroy it. Instead, think about what else could be causing the plant's unhappiness: Is there enough lighting? Do you have the right amount of water at hand? Is the temperature or humidity in the room suitable for your plant?

Take the time to figure out just what your plant needs and you will be able to estimate a right plan of action. Before fertilizing your new indoor plants, wait at least a month and always dilute the solution to the recommended proportion.

8. Don't Move Your Healthy Plant

If your new plant seems to be flourishing in a specific place, don't move it! If you move certain plants, such as Ficuses, away from their preferred locations, there is a good chance they will respond negatively. Large plants are especially vulnerable. If you do relocate your plant, make sure it has similar lighting, humidity, and temperature variations in its new location.

Purchasing a new plant is a thrilling experience that can provide you with many long-term benefits. Simply follow these eight easy guidelines to ensure that your new purchase is going to be stress-free and that you prevent typical mistakes, and you will be able to reap the beauty and health benefits that your houseplants bring.

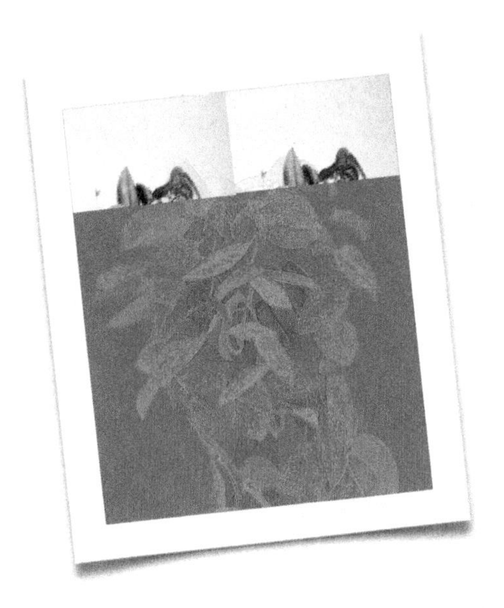

CONCLUSION

Owing a plant, and hosting it in our home, is an act of love.

Love them, and they will love you back. But plants, like humans, need to be understood. We, people, fall deep in love and are able to develop a relationship when we understand the other, and as we feel we are understood. What makes human relations matter is empathy, which means putting ourself in somebody's else shoes.

The same should be done with our plants. Let's really take a look at them and give it a try in understanding them. How are they feeling? Are they thirsty? Are they cold? Are they comfortable? It may sound a little too much but I feel that we should treat our green friends at least as we treat our pets.

The book you just read is a collection of my notes, the information that I gathered from studying the the subject and my experience. I also have many other plants, and vegetables, outside in the open, - and I invite you to check out my other books about them - but the plants that I regularly keep in my house are like old friends and make my house my home. Without them it would be very different.

I hope you have found this book helpful,

Love each other,

Christo

CHRISTO SULLIVAN

FOR BEGINNERS

TABLE OF CONTENT

INTRODUCTION

This handbook is for you to have a comprehensive 360° view on what you can do and what you can't do when you're starting your journey in the houseplant realm.

My name is Christo Sullivan and this is my second contribution to the indoor gardening literature, namely the house plants, the wonderfully green friends that we can host in our houses and can help us to relax, shoo away stress, and reconnect with Nature, even if we are living in a busy and bustling city, or - as I call them - urban nightmare.

In this book I'm going to cut the fuss, and go directly to the nitty and gritty of the house plants domain: the plants.

You can practice indoor gardening as a passion, as a hobby, even as a profession, but the common denominator is to have fun, to use the company of our green companions as a happy relief-corner of our life. If you grow your plants in the right way - which means, with the right mindset - I promise you they will make you a plant enthusiast, if you're not one yet.

CHAPTER 1

Make it Beautiful

Indoor gardening is in fact a form of horticulture therapy in which the medicinal effects of indoor plants serve the contemporary women and men that need an assistance with everyday's life. As the term "indoor garden" indicates, it refers to a garden that can be built indoors. Indoor gardens are very democratic, as they can be built really anywhere, wether you live in villa, or a tiny flat, that you want to green-up a residential or commercial structure, such as hotels, hospitals, and business offices. Indoor plants are used to decorate all kinds of interior spaces.

This gives us a strong weapon, to embellish make any environment healthy for our body and our spirit too. And of course I am not forgetting the aesthetic part of the deal. How we arrange the plants in our houses matters, because it's where we live, so it makes only sense to use a little of sense of beauty (or what we consider so) and maximize our interiors. Indoor plants may be arranged in a variety of ways, either in appropriate combinations or as a single specimen item. There are some general rules, or better, guidelines that one could follow, for example, a group of large bold-leaved plants should be positioned against a large wall in a large space. On the other hand, single plant collections work well in small rooms. Tall plants, such as philodendrons and rubber plants, are better suited to rooms with horizontal lines, while tall monstera plants and big ferns are best suited to rooms with clear straight lines in a contemporary style. Ficus, diffenbachia, and dracaena are ideal for a classic style room with ornate furnishings. Or think an amaryllis or chrysanthemum plants with red, yellow, or orange flowers; they are ideal for rooms with a white or light colored backdrop. Plants with brightly colored leaves, such as coleus and caladium, can also work well in those spaces. And some things just ask for some logic and common sense: for instance plants with white flowers work well in rooms with dark backgrounds, but also plants with variegated leaves, such as caladium, will make a beautiful, yet more subtle, contrast.

If what you are after is a visual effect of he exploitation of the tridimensionality of a specific space, you should probably consider using ferns that can be easily grouped together to achieve a great effect, and if the group includes different varieties what is created is an even greater visual texture. If you want some color you should go for a group of different varieties of begonias that you can group together to achieve an explosion of colorful armony.

So you may understand how grouping can be a perfect combo for an augmented visual experience, when you have the right plant. Specific plant height must be taken into account when grouping indoor plants for dark corners of rooms. Tall plants are placed in the rear, medium tall plants in the center, and dwarf trailing plants in the front. Spacially, tall plants should be placed in the center of a hall or room, medium tall plants should be grouped around tall plants, and dwarf plants should be placed along the perimeter. I this way you're goin to give your "little forest" an harmonious beginning, middle, and end. Potted chrysanthemums, potted asters, potted coleus, and caladium are excellent choices for such arrangements. Plants grown in terrariums and glass cases, plants grown in bottles, cups, dishes and troughs, and aquarium cases are the best indoor plants for table decorations. Indoor plants may be used to create miniature gardens inside your home. Miniature landscapes such as forest scenes, desert scenes, and formal garden scenes can be produced using the right mix of vegetation and flowering plants. If you want to put in some scenographic effort, your imagination is your only limit.Indoor plants can be presented in stunning combinations, and can make any ambience of your house special: floors, window sills and ledges, tables and desks, book cases and book shelves, shelves and trolleys, window boxes or planters.

Everything is better in three

A well known rule of (green) thumb for styling any space is to avoid grouping items together in even numbers. An even number transmits symmetry, which often brings a degree of formality which in my experience is seldom the most adapt to a home where you want to live and relax. The best way to group plants together is in odd numbers, 3, 5, 7... Or just one single plant that make a corner or a coffee table precious in its simplicity. For the same reason you should generally avoid grouping plants with the same, uniform, height. This conformation will cause the plants to blend together taking out of each plant its uniqueness. My suggestion is to include at least one plant in each group which is considerably taller than the others. Another useful advice about grouping is to try to put together plants which have something in common, a salient visual quality such as the color of their leaves, their density, their direction. Having a common visual theme adds to the natural feeling of the bunch, avoiding the risk to look randomly put together.

This is something that is often ignored, but can make a huge difference in the visual. The texture of the leaves, their physical composition, plays a subtle but substantial role in the general impression you can have of a corner of a living room if the plants used in a group varies in structure and consistency. When two plants or two version of the same plants are paired, it's important to think in terms of contrast, such as rough versus smooth or detailed versus minimal.

Play with Texture

The advice here is, if you have minimalistic interiors, a plant with a more intricate appearance, with many peculiar details that can be noticed even fro afar, will make the ambience multi-dimensional, so that we can appreciate both the two contrasting style together. An example of plant to obtain this could be Maranta Leuconeira or a Zanzibar Gem. If, on the other hand, your house is already full of texture and detailed garnishes a plain yet elegant big glossy leaf is what you should go for in order to regain the room's balance, like the elegant Red Congo.

Something else you have control upon arranging plants is the "flatness" of a room. Depending on the height of your plants you have the freedom to explore the eye level or higher. Taller plants are usually displayed o the ground level, while smaller plants can be placed on a shelf or hanging from the ceiling, giving you the chance to use the space also in its verticality. On a shelf for example one of the best thing you can have is a trailing plant, like a cascading photos; it's vines will grow out to create an abundant jungle-like feel. You can also use plant stands to help the plant look to stand out in its vertical, especially when its color is contrasting.

The single trait that I deem the most important in the houseplants in a room however, especially for that first glance that you throw to a room when you first enter it, is... the direction of where the leaves grow. Using the leading lines of a plant's leaves is a great way to lead direction toward a retina area of the room. There are some plants whose leaves point naturally to the ceiling, and lead the eye up, like the famous snake plant. On the contrary, the eye is drawn downward by pants with trailing vines, like those within the photos and Philodendron families. Their mantles are perfect to bring attention to a fireplace or any other key furniture piece.

Lastly, try to balance the colors in your room with that of your plants. If you have a group of three plants you may want to try a primary color, a secondary color and the smallest of them with a vivid bold color, to add just a splash of sparkly note, for example with a fluorescent - and contained - yellow. Or what about the pink details of a rubber tree?
A different discussion should be made about the vase, containers or planters that you're going to use. Also them play a relevant role, and you can play around with the many different options that you can find on the market.

The last fundamental piece of advice is that no plant is as beautiful as a thriving plant. The most important thing you can do for your plants to look good, is to treat them in the proper way. Make them happy, and they'll make you happy as well.

CHAPTER
2

Houseplant Profile

You can't wait to start your journey into the houseplants world. I can't blame you. In fact I believe you have already started one. The greens are in the house. So, what's next? You want your plants to thrive, how do you make it happen? First, you have to determine what kind of plant do you have. Depending on the plant type you have purchased - or that you are about to buy - the condition of light, watering, climate, how it grows and how it can be repotted, may change. From here you can determine what's the best way to care for it. What follows is a list of what I consider the best plants you can take care of if you're not an expert, but you still want to fill your house with plants. Easy enough, but at the same time beautiful, curious, and make great decoration for your house.

If you're new to plant caring, this is a perfect place to start. If you've been caring for plants for a while, this could be a good refresher. Here we go.

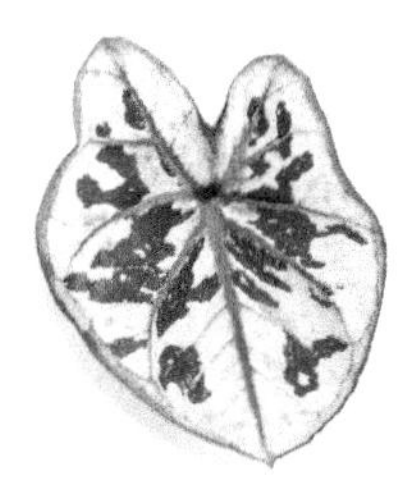
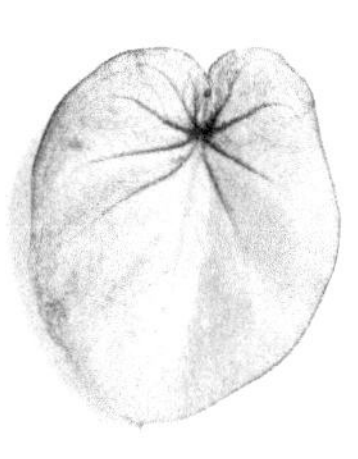
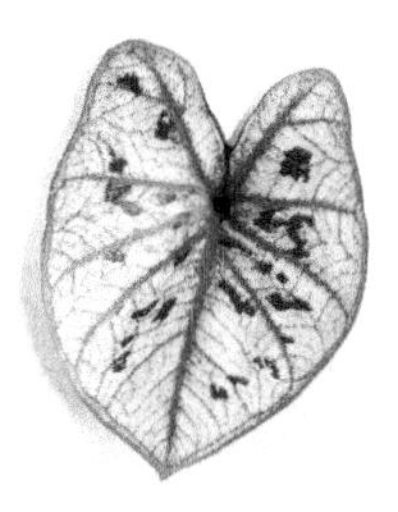

MACULATA BEGONIA

(Indoor Polkadot Plant)

Polka dot Begonia, the maculata, is a real eyecatcher.

Place it on a design table, or against a backdrop with geometrical or minimalistic features, and with its large olive green angel wing-shaped leaves patterned with polka dots on top and a deep purple-red on the bottom side, it will draw on her everybody's attention. The best part is that with this houseplant, you don't need a green thumb to impress. They are very permissive and will live with little or no effort on your part.

Begonia plants come in a variety of styles, heights, and shapes, as well as hybrids. The Begonia maculata is a fast-growing plant that makes a great indoor houseplant or terrarium plant, and is without a doubt one of the most beautiful Begonia plants I've ever seen, that's why she's the first of our list.

TRUST ME: ***get one and you will already feel halfway on your path to become a plant-expert***

Indoor Polkadot Plant Care Guide

LIGHT

Bright, indirect sunlight is ideal for Begonia maculata. It is possible for her, however, to expand also in low-light conditions. Keep the plant out of the intense early afternoon sun; the leaves of the polka dot begonia will burn and dry out if they are exposed to too much sunlight.

While light is essential, the humidity factor is the key to begonia maculata treatment. Its native habitat is a steamy setting, which doesn't mean you will need to build a greenhouse for it, but you will have to allow for some humidity to keep your maculata happy and healthy. A sad clown begonia is the last thing anyone needs.

WATERING

Since the Begonia maculata don't like to be left dry for long periods of time, it should be watered on a daily basis. It prefers a damp soil setting, keep an eye out, however, for soggy seeds, which won't help the plant's well-being at all. Becasue of that, before watering, let the top of the soil dry out. Let it drain in full before placing the pot back on the saucer or in its cache pot.

The Begonia maculata may need to be watered more often when it is vigorously growing in the spring and summer, as the temperatures are higher and the sun rays intake is much more.

In the winter, it can be challenging to understand their watering needs. Simply water your begonia less and less often while checking the soil. The Begonia maculata does not go dormant in the winter, but it does slow down considerably. It still needs to be watered though, so make sure to keep on watering it regularly also during he winter. Don't let your good intentions hurt your beautiful plant; learn to listen her.

FLOWERING

You can find blooms on a single stem from spring to fall, that will tend to form clusters of white flowers with cheery yellow centers. Just beautiful, and one of my wife's favorites.

REPOTTING

Since this plant tends to be root attached, the best growing condition for it would be in a smaller container. Don't be tempted to repot it too fast because it thrives in small spaces.

When it's time to repot, do so in the spring when the plant is only starting to expand and will be ready to fit into its new container. Make sure the new pot is one size larger than the old one and has drainage holes to save the plant from getting root rot.

AFRICAN VIOLET

Since it is native to Africa and the flowers resemble violets (though they are unrelated), the Saint-paulia houseplant is also known as the African Violet. This plant is a relatively recent addition to our homes, having first appeared in vast quantities in America in the 1930s, but It has been well-received ever since.

African violets are among the most common houseplants in the world, and for good reason. These low-growing, compact plants bloom several times a year and come in a variety of leaf shapes and colors. Don't let their reputation for complexity deter you: African violets will excel indoors if you foll ow a few basic guidelines.

TRUST ME: ***With a little practice, you can keep them in bloom almost all year and raise them to be the size of dinner plates.***

African Violet Care Guide

LIGHT

Always keep your African Violet out of direct sunshine. If you want to make flowers, you'll need a lot of sun. The plant will move to a shadier place, but this will result in a longer time between flowering periods.

WATERING

Enable the compost to dry out somewhat between watering to keep it moist. While many people recommend only watering from the bottom, if you are smart, you should water from the tip. Slow down so you don't splash the leaves, which will spoil their velvety appearance and greatly raise the risk of multiple fungal infections.

HUMIDITY

The plant prefers high humidity, but you should avoid misting it to increase humidity in case it's too low, since this will often damp the leaves way too much. Instead, try some of our other suggestions to avoid problems caused by too-wet leaves.

FERTILIZING

Use a high-potash feed if possible, or an all-purpose houseplant variety if that isn't possible. If you decide to enrich your household with African Violet flowers, you'll need to feed them every couple of weeks. Reduce the feeding schedule if you are not supplying the required bright (but indirect) light so the plant would not need it.Temperatures the Violet is comfortable in range from 60°F to 72°F (15°C to 21°C). In the winter, try to maintain the temperature above 60°F / 15°C.

REPOTTING

Again, don't go on a repotting spree. If you do it too often, you may reduce the flowering capacity, as a slightly plant-bound pot aids in the blooming process. Repotting is needed for very young plants or mature plants that are too pot-bound, preferably in the spring or early summer.

AGLAONEMA

(Chinese Evergreens)

Aglaonema, or Chinese Evergreens, are decorative foliage houseplants that flourish in our homes and offices. They're great for beginners because they tolerate low light and intermittent maintenance, but they're still appealing to seasoned gardeners.

True, they don't have the same wow factor as some other indoor plants, but Chinese Evergreens are incredibly understated, and they're one of the best plants to make every office more relaxed with a touch of elegance. In fact they are a great addition to any classic style home.

They grow slowly and take a long time to outgrow their containers, so they need little upkeep. They're tough and, for the most part, laid-back. In reality, they're among the least fussy houseplants available.

TRUST ME: ***Aglaonema plants in general are extremely adaptable to a wide range of indoor environmental growth conditions.***

Indoor Polkadot Plant Care Guide

LIGHT

These plants are ideal for mild, medium, and bright light environments in your house. They'll add a splash of color and flourish in places where other houseplants could suffer. They won't live in complete darkness, so don't even think about placing it in a room with no windows.

According to conventional wisdom, Aglaonema species with light green or highly variegated foliage need more light than those with darker green and less variegation. You won't go wrong if you follow this rule.

WATERING

These plants prefer a slightly damp / moist soil. So don't allow it to neither be wet soil or go completely dry. In the winter, if your plant is in a low-lig-ht setting, you can only need to water it once every two weeks. Watering once or twice a week might be needed in lighter light or if the temperature is extremely hot.

While these plants are very low maintenance, there's a possibility for things to go wrong by mistake when it comes to watering. These are the symptoms to watch for and what they mean.

- Drooping leaves and wet soil meanshe plant is over-watered.
- Leaves and stems pointing very upright along with dry soil mean the plant is under-watered.

HUMIDITY

Since these plants are tough, if given the option, they would choose high humidity, but they can also cope with low humidity. They won't thrive if the air in your home or office is very dry, so keep that in mind.

REPOTTING AND SOIL

Plants of the genus Aglaonema mature slowly and compactly. As a result, they take a long time to outgrow a pot. Of course, this will happen naturally, but if the plant seems to be particularly congested or hasn't produced new growth in a long time, it's probably time to repot it.

They'll thrive in a number of growing mediums, so you can probably use anything you already have on hand. If you're buying something new, it'll probably be cheaper and easier to stick to the basics and opt for something labelled for houseplants or garden plants.

TILLANDSIA AIR PLANTS

This little plant is a beauty, and as a low-maintenance houseplant, Tillandsia Air Plants are quickly gaining popularity. They don't need to be grown in soil pots because they have such a small root system. Air Plants may be hung, mounted, or set in terrariums, bottle gardens, or other decorative containers with grit, stones, or pretty much anything else. Air plants are ideal for craft designs, small-space living, and ultimately, bragging rights for brown-thumb gardeners. Superglue their roots to stones or wood, or tuck them into shells and driftwood crevices, glass baubles, and wire baskets. Place them between the leaves or around the base of your larger houseplants. They make ideal companions for orchids, cactus and bromeliads. Alternatively, simply place them unadorned on a sunny windowsill or shelf.

Air Plant Care Guide

LIGHT

According to popular belief, all Air Plants need bright light with a little direct sunlight every now and then. However, depending on the variety, I've discovered that Air Plants can thrive under a variety of light conditions. The natural color of the Air Plant is a good starting point. The color spectrum begins with dark green and progresses through light green, grey, and finally to almost white variations.

The green ones would do well in places with little sun, all the way up to some bright spots on window ledges. They don't like direct sunshine, though.

WATERING

Watering Air Plants can be done in two ways. The first step is to mist the leaves two or three times a week. If the plant is set in place which is difficult to reach this is a good option.

Dunk your Air Plant in a bottle with room temperature water as a second choice. Some argue that a dunk is insufficient and that the plant should be soaked in the container for at least half hour.

I don't really disagree, particularly if you live in a dry climate or your plant is severely dehydrated. However, soaking it in this manner on a daily basis makes caring for these plants even more complex and time intensive than it needs to be.

Instead, I think that dunking them in the container for no longer than 15 seconds before extracting them and shaking off the excess water, makes them completely content.

It's crucial to shake off any extra water to have enough time for the plant to fully dry before nightfall as the temperature decreases. There is a risk of decay if there is too much moisture on the plant and the temperature lowers. As a general rule, water early in the morning rather than late at night.

HUMIDITY

This may be crucial. Dark to light green air plants need more regular watering and a higher humidity level than grey air plants.

You should be good if you can mist or soak once or twice a week, and you should be able to ignore humidity. If watering that much is a challenge for you, the humidity must be kept at a reasonable level to keep the balance.

REPOTTING

The wonderful trait of not having any sort of extensive root system means this is one of the very few houseplants that will never need repotting.

Speed of Growth. The Tillandsia grow rapidly at first, but then it slows down, state that will persist for the remainder of the plant's life. Whatever you do for your Tillandsia, don't expect it to grow quickly.

ALOCASIA

(Kris Plant / Elephant Ear)

The Kris Plant, Elephant Ear, and African Mask Plant are both names for Alocasia. This unusual-looking houseplant will occasionally bloom, but it's usually not bought for that purpose. The peculiarity of the Alocasia is all about the rare and alien-like leaves.

Look at them, they will make any ambience special. The striking leaves are arrowhead or shield shaped, with long protruding white veins running across them, which contrast sharply with the dark green leaf.

Alocasia Care Guide

Alocasia is not tough to grow, but it is probably one of the most demanding plant in this list, because ti will not tolerate poor treatment or poor conditions over extended periods of time.

LIGHT

You should keep your plant out of direct sunlight as well as from places that are very dark and gloomy. It is important to find locations that are halfway between these two extremes. In our experience, two species of Alocasia, Zebrina and Mycorrhiza, cope much better with morning or late afternoon sun dropping on their leaves than the Amazonica species, that deals better with extended exposure to sunlight.

WATERING

When the compost is in active development, it must be kept moist at all times. That's not dry or soggy; it's sticky. The roots of the Elephant Plant hate being dry, but too much water can cause them to rot.

Rather than following traditional houseplant watering advice, we've discovered that the best approach is to water little. If you want to reserve her a special trearment, make an attempt to use tepid rainwater if possible.

HUMIDITY

Another explanation for this plant's growing failure in a home setting is the lack of moisture in the air. It's a tropical plant that needs moderate to high humidity.

REPOTTING

Repotting in the spring isn't always needed, but if your plant has developed a lot of offsets or has outgrown its container, it could be a good idea. While they seem to be tropical and unique species, you can use any regular houseplant compost or blend.

SPEED OF GROWTH

In summer, when the days are long and the temperature is high, expect a moderate rate of development. One new leaf each month is reasonably normal; marginally less is also acceptable and not cause for concern. If you have not spot any new leaves in 6 months, you can consider repotting or fertilizing (if you haven't already).

ALOE BARBADENSIS

(Aloe Vera)

Because of the Aloe Vera gel found within its leaves, the Aloe Barbadensis plant is one of the most well-known houseplants.

Aloe vera is a well-known medicinal plant that has been used by humans for thousands of years. It includes antioxidant and antibacterial elements as well as beneficial plant compounds. If you want to improve your health, you may even grow them and learn to extract the Aloe substance. I suggest that you try and bring half a glass of it every morning, You'd be surprised of the benefits.

Aloe Vera Care Guide

LIGHT

Your Aloe Vera plant will thrive in every South-facing window because it will get plenty of sunlight. It's simply built for such places, like most succulents, and as a result, you'll get good quality leaves and an even growth.

However, Aloes will resist also in a north-facing location; only, growth will be slower, and you'll need to change the plant pot every month or two to maintain an even appearance. When it comes to light, the Aloe Vera plant is generally adaptable, and once it's growing it's very difficult to stop.

WATERING

During the spring and summer, water thoroughly if the soil becomes dry. The location of the plant will determine how long it takes for the soil to dry out and, as a result, how long you would go between waterings. It's perfectly normal to wait anywhere from a week to three weeks.

In hot weather, aloes can use a lot of water, so don't be afraid to water them. Water less often in the Fall and Winter. Some people don't water their plants at all during the winter, which, if they're in a particularly cool place, is usually a smart thing to avoid root/stem rot. During winter your Aloe will start to suffer only if temperature goes below 30F.

HUMIDITY

Almost all succulents, including the Aloe Vera vine, do not need much humidity.

REPOTTING

Aloe Vera plants typically grow a large number of offsets or suckers in a short period of time, eventually filling the jar. When the pot gets overcrowded, repot.

If you want a "busy" look, hold all of the plants together in a larger container, or separate any of the offsets for propagation or gifting.

SPEED OF GROWTH

In ideal conditions, your Aloe Vera plant can grow at a moderate pace. If conditions are bad, and, of course, during the winter months when everything slows down, expect very little development.

HEIGHT / SPREAD

They are usually just 45cm / 18in high. However, because of the offsets that fan out around, if you one day decide to plant it outside, in that case the spread (over several years) can be enormous.

DYPSIS LUTESCENS

(Areca Palm / Butterfly Palm)

The Areca Palm, also known as the Butterfly Palm, is a low-maintenance houseplant which has a lot to offer. This lovely Nature's masterpiece has earned the "Royal Horticultural Society's Award of Garden Merit", which is quite an accomplishment for a plant that is more widely grown indoors than outdoors. Because of its narrow, multiple fronds spaced close to one another in tidy compact lines along the stems, it can easily be distinguished from other varieties of palms. It's an "airy" plant that can give you the impression of an elegant urban forest; 3 or 4 of them lined in two rows can really give a pleasant tridimensional look to the green in your house.

Areca Palm Care Guide

LIGHT

Areca palms can grow in a spot that receives no sunshine at all during the day as well as one which is exposed to direct sunlight, but they don't like excessive quantities of either. It's best to stay away from very dim shady areas and constant direct sunshine. The best possible position we can place it is a spot which is sunny, but that gets no direct sunlight; or alternatively a spot that receives just a limited amount of direct light during the morning or the evening.

WATERING

Areca Palms are tropical native plants, and they're genetically used to frequent tropical rains, and to having their roots in perpetually moist soil. And this is exactly how we should keep them when we choose to keep this plant in our homes: we will need to keep the soil moist for long periods of time. This palm is thirsty in the spring, summer, and autumn/fall, necessitating frequent and heavy watering especially throughout the summer. If the location you have selected for the Areca is really hot, you might need to water it twice a week. Despite its thirst for moisture, too much water can easily destroy your plant. It's better to wait until the surface soil has dried before watering again. An occasional draught can be tolerated by the plant, but you should not keep its soil dry for more than a couple days.

REPOTTING

Since palms dislike constant root disturbance, frequent repotting will harm your Areca and prevent its growth. However, since they don't grow very quickly and don't like being in smaller pots with their roots crowded, repotting isn't something you should be doing very often. I'd say once every couple of years is enough, but if your plant happens to be very young, as it grows you'll be repotting it once a year in the Spring, before it matures. When it comes to doing it, regular potting soil would suffice.

HEIGHT / SPREAD

It can reach generous height, but few indoor specimens would ever grow to be more than 10 ft (3 m) tall.

BIRD'S NEST FERN

(Asplenium Nidus)

Asplenium nidus, or Bird's Nest Fern, is one of many common and attractive ferns that can be easily grown as houseplants. Ferns such as this one thrive next to windows facing North, which is the best one for its quality of light and correct average temperature.

The Bird's Nest Fern will reward you with a large number of naturally glossy leaves arranged in a circular pattern that resembles a bird's nest (hence the common name for these houseplants)

Bird Nest Fern Care Guide

LIGHT

The Bird's Nest Fern needs only medium light levels to grow strong, which makes it more durable in less warmer enviroments. If you have a North-facing windows you should have one of this plant in front of it.

If you don't have such a spot or if your rooms don't face North, just keep it out of the sunlight and you'll be fine.

WATERING

You should not allow the soil to dry out at all during the growing process; instead, keep it only damp.

The first reason why ferns often die in homes is the way they are watered, either too much or too little. Although an occasional mistake is appropriate, you can continue to work with your Fern by keeping the soil just moist during the growing seasons (Spring, Summer, and Autumn/Fall).

HUMIDITY

The plant needs a high level of humidity to survive, which is why it thrives in humid terrariums, sunrooms, and conservatories.

Of course, you can grow a smaller plant without specialized equipment. Just know that id the ambience is dry you should add a humidifier somewhere near your plant.

REPOTTING

When the thin roots entirely fill the existing jar, it's time to repot; if this happens, it's time to transfer it to a somewhat larger tub. If you don't, the growth will slow down and finally end.

A young Bird Nest Fern plant should be repotted once a year until it reaches a good height (around 1.5ft), after which it should only need repotting every couple of years.

You don't need to use or do something overly fancy while you're repotting your fern. Standard potting soil will do, and if the roots are very compacted, gently loosen them with your fingertips.

. Height / Spread

After several years, a maximum height of 4ft / 120cm and a spread of 3ft / 90cm can be achieved, but only in a very humid climate. Half these size estimates in a normal room.

BIRD OF PARADISE

(Strelitzia)

The spectacular, unmistakable, and unchallenged Queen of the houseplant world is the Strelitzia, also known as the Bird of Paradise Plant. When it's in bloom, the flowers resemble the head of an exotic crested duck, which is how it got its common name.

Sunbirds pollinate the flowers by perching on the "beak" ledge of the flower. The weight of the bird on the "beak" opens it, allowing pollen to fall onto the bird and be deposited on the next flower it visits. Just magical.

Bird of Paradise Care Guide

LIGHT

You'll need bright light and some sun if you want a lot of growth and this wonderful plant's flowers. A window with an east or west orientation should suffice. It's also a good idea to choose a south-facing window if you want some protection from the hot summer sun, which can roast the leaves of immature plants.

North-facing location should be avoided if you plan to keep the Strelitzia there for a long time. It will tolerate a darker location for a while, but in that case its development will be much slower, and flowering unlikely. So the best solution is to give her some south-facing exposure initially, and place it next to an east or west facing window When the plant is strong enough.

WATERING

The amount of water required will be determined by the location of your plant. Plants in lighter, colder locations would need significantly more than those in darker locations. The usual reasonable rule of thumb - watering when the surface of the soil turns dry - is valid here. I have 3 Strelitzia and one tip I use to understand if they have enough water is one that you can use with any plant that can stay in a small pot: lift it and "feel" its weight. After a while you will develop a feel for when to water just by the weight of the pot. The less the water I the pots, the lighter they will be.

HUMIDITY

If the air is very dry, a light misting can help to remove the dust that colle-cts on the leaves. For my experience humidity is not an essential condition for this plant to grow.

REPOTTING

When the Strelitzia is young, it is perfectly fine to repot each Spring using normal potting compost. However if you want flowers or you're trying to restrict the growth of the plant you need to keep it pot-bound. If it's housed in a plastic pot, a large Bird of Paradise will eventually distort and bulge it horribly. As a result, be prepared to cut it loose while repotting, and be aware that doing so would most likely interrupt the flowering period.

SPEED OF GROWTH

In ideal conditions, Bird of Paradise growth is rapid, with one new leaf appearing per month during the growing season. While it does not seem to be anything at first glance, the dense roots under the soil surface are genuinely thick and can quickly fill a pot, making this a fast-growing plant.

BOSTON FERN

(Nephrolepis Exaltata 'Bostoniensis')

The Boston Fern is a perfect plant to keep indoors to recalls the nature outside. A variety of Nephrolepis is a good choice if you want a dependable and relatively easy-to-care-for fern.

The Boston Fern has elegant green, drooping fronds that are naturally shaped in such a way that they seem ruffled, making it look great in a hanging basket or anywhere the fronds can hang down from, such as the edge of a bookcase or shelf.

Boston ferns (Nephrolepis exaltata) are now common houseplants because of their tridimensionality and the joy they can bring to a living room or a kitchen. Place it on a coffee table and they will lighten the room up right away.

Boston Fern Care Guide

LIGHT

It is important to provide adequate lighting. A Boston Fern can tolerate both full sun and partial shade, but for a happy and good-looking plant, choose a sunny spot that does not receive direct sunshine.

A window that faces north will be perfect. If looking east (or west in a pinch) is also appropriate, facing south in direct sunlight should be avoided.

WATERING

In the winter the soil should be almost always damp, just spray when its surface is dry. In hot weather, on the other hand, you may comfortably water this plant several days a week.

Moisture is essential, but don't overwater to the point that the soil becomes saturated and sodden. If you can, use rain water, but if it isn't possible, tap water would suffice. Only make sure it's been able to stay for an hour at room temperature, as very cold water will shock the roots.

REPOTTING

Repot only if you want the plant to grow larger, and even then, only after the roots have fully filled the original container. Make a special effort to keep the fern at the same soil level as before. It's important not to bury the crown, as this would make it rot and lead the plant to its inevitable demise.

SPEED OF GROWTH

When conditions are favorable, expect fast and consistent development for the majority of the year. In colder temperatures, or in case the roots have run out of room to develop, growth can considerably slow down.

HEIGHT / SPREAD

After several years, this fern can reach a maximum height of 3ft / 90cm and a spread of 6ft / 180cm.

CACTUS

(Desert Cacti)

Here is one of the plants that I suggest most often to people asking me what plant should they get to keep at home with no, or little, effort. The Desert Cacti have the same lighting, humidity, and watering specifications as other cacti. They never outgrow their spot in your home or their pots, are inexpensive to buy (when young), and only require simple care.

When compared to other houseplants, even if your thumb doesn't look anything like green and you are an undercover houseplants killer, a cactus will usually take more blows before succumbing. On the other hand, if you pay close attention, you will have a lovely peaceful companion rising happily, and maybe producing some lovely flowers.

Cactus Care Guide

LIGHT

In the vast majority of instances, a cactus can thrive in a position that enjoys direct sunshine for half or most part of the day. If your cactus can bloom indoors it will with this kind of light, but not all of them do. Almost all cacti, though, will tolerate a shadier spot for a while, but their growth will suffer. Think where they come from, shower them with light.

WATERING

The most frequent cactus misconception is that "they don't need much water". From one point of view, yes, this is absolutely correct; no other plant is as well suited to withstand prolonged drought. If you fail to water the soil after it has dried out, it will most likely live for several weeks, if not months, without damage, which makes it so versatile.

However, the plant has now become a survivor rather than a thriver as a result of this. Instead, the perfect time to water your cactus is when the soil has fully dried out from the last watering. When this occurs, re-water thoroughly and then stop giving until the soil has dried out again.

REPOTTING

Despite their ultimate size, most cacti have a small root volume relative to what can be seen above ground. Since the roots of small plants are mostly shallow rather than deep, using a wide container for them to "build into" is often a mistake, since it greatly raises the chance of overwatering and rotting.

Every year or so, young plants would need to be repotted to give the roots room to mature. You will reduce the frequency to 3 or 5 years cycles until it reaches a significant scale. For a very tall or mature cactus, you'll need a good solid and heavy container to keep it from toppling over. Many cactus growers suggest clay pots because they are porous and allow the roots to "breathe," but you can use plastic if you prefer. If you're repotting a cactus on a regular basis, make sure it gets fertilized.

ARE CACTUS PLANTS POISONOUS?

There are several different types of cacti to choose from, and some of them are toxic to both humans and pets. If they have thorns, claws, or spines, though, they shouldn't be a concern so you can keep curious children and pets safe (it's obviously advisable to not touch them).

SCHLUMBERGERA BUCKLEYI

(Christmas Cactus/Thanksgiving cactus)

The Christmas cactus is a very popular houseplant for a reason: they grow bright, tubular beautiful flowers in pink or lilac colors when they bloom. They're a fantastic plant because of their lovely flowers, long bloom time, and low maintenance requirements. I'm sure you'd love a Christmas cactus in your house!

Christmas Cactus Care Guide

LIGHT

The Christmas Cactus, unlike desert cacti, is native to shady forests. This ensures that clear, bright sunlight should be avoided, otherwise the leaves could turn to a reddish, almost damaged color. They need a well-lit area, but they may accept darker conditions if clearer light can be provided for at least a few months of the year. Direct sunlight must be avoided, which is unusual for cacti.

WATERING

Like all cacti they can store water in their thick fleshy leaves and rely on it in times of drought. However, if you want your specimen to thrive, you'll need to water it like a regular houseplant, anytime the soil becomes dry. Water the plant thoroughly and wait until the top inch or so of soil has dried out before watering it again. I've never seen one of these plants succumb to root rot as a result of overwatering, so they seem to be resistant to root rot, but I would avoid overwatering just in case.

TEMPERATURE

The average temperature present in most households shouldn't be a problem for our plant. After it has flowered, it needs to rest at a somewhat colder temperature, between 7°C and 16°C (45°F and 61°F). In most cases, an unheated space would be preferable. Sub-zero temperatures can be avoided at all costs.

REPOTTING

The Christmas Cactus grows steadily and takes a long time (years and years!) to become pot bound. If necessary, repot after flowering, but you shouldn't have to do it more than once every three years or so.

When it's time to repot it, just use a similar potting mix to the one it's currently in. This should be something relatively "open", such as regular potting soil or something specifically labelled for cactus and succulent plants. Since the root system is usually simple and not excessively vigorous, choose a pot that is only marginally larger than the previous one if you're also removing the growing container.

SPEED OF GROWTH

As houseplants, these plants mature at a slow pace. However, if the conditions are favorable, they will continue to grow at a reasonable rate, and you will see a lot of fresh light green growth in the growing season.

ARE CHRISTMAS PLANTS POISONOUS?

Although the leaves and flowers are unpleasant to the taste, the plant is not poisonous to humans, cats, or dogs.

PLECTRANTHUS SCUTELLARIOIDES

(Coleus Blumei)

Coleus Blumei hybrids, also known as Painted Nettles or Plectranthus scutellarioides in Latin, are historically cultivated as outdoor bedding plants that are handled as annuals. This ensures they're planted outdoors in late spring in order to embellish your garden during the summer and autumn, before succumbing to the frost.

If you haven't figured it out yet, the biggest selling point for these plants is the exquisitely brightly coloured and stunning leaves, some of which are marked with almost contrasting psychedelic patterns.

Coleus Care Guide

LIGHT

Coleus plants need a bright light source without direct sunlight to keep their markings, and since the leaf markings is the peculiar trait that makes this plant particularly appealing, it's critical that you get the light requirements right. Sitting squarely in a North, East, or West facing window is ideal, but, if the sunshine is filtered, you might be able to get away with a South facing window too.

Choose a bright light source that is warmed by the sun for best results.

WATERING

If you've picked a sunny spot that is automatically warmed by day light, you'll now need to keep the soil moist at all times, which might mean taking out your watering can once or twice a week. In the winter, cut back on irrigation and let the soil dry out a bit.

TEMPERATURE

Provide an average temperature of no less than 50°F (10°C), or the Coleus will perish.

REPOTTING

If you want to hold the plant alive through the winter, prune it back hard in the spring and repot it with fresh quality potting soil. You can keep the previous pot: unless you wish to maximize its total capacity, a size change is rarely necessary.

SPEED OF GROWTH

In optimal conditions, the growth rate is always very high, so you'll need to prune it on constantly to keep it compact and tidy.

HEIGHT/SPREAD

The stems will rise to 1ft - 2ft / 30cm - 60cm if left unchecked. This may be what you're aiming for but pinching out the growing tips on a regular basis will keep things shorter.

IS COLEUS POISONOUS?

Many hybrids are safe to have around people and livestock, but other varieties retain more of the "natural" characteristics of older plants. These have higher levels of essential oils in the leaves, which can induce vomiting and diarrhea if eaten in large quantities.

MUSA

(Banana Dwarf Cavendis)

Musa, also known as the banana, is one of the most well-known fruits in the world; in addition to being tasty and nutritious, several varieties can be cultivated as houseplants with ease and success.

Dwarf banana plants are often seen growing in areas of Asia for mass production, and they are often cultivated as tall demonstration plants in gardens at the back of borders to add a tropical touch. However, since they need a lot of care during winters, the average gardener is unlikely to cultivate them this way. It can seem unusual as a houseplant, but it has been grown indoors since Victorian days, when it was proudly displayed in their humid, wet, and sunny conservatories. Of course, Victorian conse-rvatories were different (and somewhat larger) than the ones we have tod-ay, but the core concept remains the same.

TRUST ME: ***This is a plant that will take everybody's attention.***

Banana Dwarf Care Guide

LIGHT

The Common Banana requires bright light, but it can tolerate a wide variety of lighting conditions, from partial shade to full sun. In full Summer sun, young plants and new leaves can scorch, particularly if your watering routine is not constant.

WATERING

During the hottest months of the year, a well-established Banana plant would need much more watering than most house plants, particularly in the Spring and Autumn/Fall. This is due to the wide leaf surface area, which makes for a great deal of transpiration, which is beneficial in the dry environment of a centrally heated home.

When the top 2 inches / 4cm of compost is dry, water it. You might be doing this as well as any other day in Summer if you're in a really light, warm place. However, if you don't cut back significantly in the winter, it's an invitation for rot to take over.

HUMIDITY

The leaves seem sturdy, but they are extremely fragile and can quickly rip if the right conditions are not met. Low humidity is a common cause of leaf destruction, so moisture-retentive pellets in the drip tray, as well as daily misting, will be beneficial.

FEEDING

Because this plant has big leaves that form quickly during the growing season, a new leaf every 10 days isn't unusual, and feeding on a regular basis is essential to keep up with the rate of the plant's development. Feed every 2 to 3 weeks with a general liquid garden fertilizer, or make your own if you choose. You should, of course, use a feed made specifically for houseplants. If the plant is overgrown and you don't want it any taller, stop fertilizing it and you want to encourage new growth.

REPOTTING

Young plants, the banana "pups," easily fill small pots, necessitating regular repotting into larger containers, perhaps twice or three times in the first year. At this stage, all you need is regular potting soil.

PROPAGATION

According to the Dwarf Cavendish's tendency for sucking, new "pups" will be born when the parent grows older. They can be gently taken away from

SCHLUMBERGERA GAERTNERI

(Easter Cactus)

The Easter cactus (also Rhipsalidopsis gaertneri) has a wide range of bloom colors. They're usually in bloom when you buy them, and they're popular holiday presents. Flowers come in a variety of colors, including white, crimson, green, peach, lavender, and pink.

The plant's peculiar appearance attracts the eye even after it has bloomed. New growth adds to the segments, giving them a rickety stacked feel. The plant lacks the spines of a desert cactus, instead taking on a more undulating shape with more pointing nodes on the leaf edges.

It has lovely knockout flowers that bloom in the months of March and April. When not in bloom, the Easter Cactus resembles the Christmas Cactus, and while both are relatively easy to care for and re-flower the following year, the Easter Cactus is less popular as a houseplant.

Easter Cactus Guide

LIGHT

Average lighting; don't expose it to heavy shadow or direct sunshine for extended periods of time. Deep shade produces no growth and few, if any, flowers. Since the Easter Cactus is not a desert cactus, it must be protected from direct sunshine. The leaves will turn reddish-brown if exposed to too much light.

WATERING

Like all cacti, they can store water in their thick fleshy leaves and survive droughts. However, if you leave the soil to dry out entirely for an extended period of time, the plant may begin to lose its leaf parts. Look for consistently damp rather than muddy soil, and use tepid rather than cool water when watering.

If the plant has been placed in a dry setting, placing the container in a pebble tray or misting the leaves a few times a month is advised (their natural habitat are shady, dank and moisture filled forests).

FEEDING

Feed once a month during the growing season with an all-purpose houseplant fertiliser.

TEMPERATURE

In most households, the average temperature is ideal for the Easter Cactus. From October to early the following year, the plant should be held in a slightly cooler (7°C - 15°C / 45°F - 59°F) climate. The most common option is an unheated space.

REPOTTING

It takes a long time for it to become pot bound because it grows slowly. If required, repot after flowering in early summer, but it's unlikely you'll need to do so more than once every few years.

SPEED OF GROWTH

During the growing season, slow but steady growth is to be expected.

HEIGHT/SPREAD

It's slow to rise, but it can stretch out over time and never get really tall.

ECHEVERIAS

Echeverias are pretty popular outdoors, but they've become very fashionable modern indoor houseplants in recent years. Despite their semi-desert origins in Central America, Mexico, and northwestern South America, they thrive as indoor plants. It's typical to see them grown in odd and visually arty pots and containers, much like many other small succulents. They're little houseplants, similar to the Haworthia, and they're always easy and quick to care for. You can go a month without watering them and they won't be too upset. However, to really make them shine, you must properly care for them.

The leaves come in a variety of shades, ranging from basic greens to more vibrant hues. These leaves usually develop a rosette pattern that stays with them throughout their whole existence.

The rosette shape allows for optimum light penetration while still allowing the plants to easily absorb and direct water down to the roots. Tehre are several reason why you may want an Echeveria in your house: first of all, it's hard to mess up with Echeverias so they make excellent plants for beginners. They make great presents and they are inexpensive (in truth, some of the rarer hybrids are expensive, but the more common types are really cheap to buy). Maintenance is easy and growth is slow even in ideal conditions, so that you may only need to repot it once every few years.

TRUST ME: ***They are unique looking and frequently sold in stylish containers, they make super convenient birthday gifts that will leave a positive impression for years to come.***

Echeveria Care Guide

LIGHT

Almost all Echeveria plants thrive in bright, indirect sunlight. They struggle in low light and with persistent direct intense sunshine, especially if your watering skills aren't up to par.

Window ledges are ideal for your Echeveria, but if you want to keep one with a southern exposure, give it some shielding and move it as soon as you see any damage. Burned leaves do not heal, and since they expand slowly and retain their leaves for long periods, the burn can last a long time.

WATERING

Many succulents in the wild have evolved to heavy rains followed by a long period of time before the next one occurs. Many of their characteristics, such as their thick fleshy leaves and the way they funnel water directly to the roots, aid in this.

Echeverias appreciate a strong deep watering every now and then, followed by a wait before they dry out entirely or mostly. They aren't cacti, so they shouldn't be dehydrated for long periods of time. As a general rule, during the Spring and Summer, water deeply and often if the soil seems to be drying out. Water less deeply and wait until the soil dries out completely from late Fall to early Winter.

Watering them from above and through the middle of the plant is perfectly acceptable, even though many people would advise you not to. The primary explanation for this belief is that if water "sits" in the rosette it could remain there for hours, if not days, rotting the plant's central portion. Don't let your plant live in such conditions.

HUMIDITY

These are not tropical plants, despite being simple houseplants. Indoors, their biggest flaw is a lack of decent, consistent ventilation combined with extremely humid conditions. Such conditions will increase the likelihood of your plant rotting rapidly. Choose a spot that allows for some natural ventilation, such as near a window. However, attempting to cultivate it in a continuously steamy environment such as a bathroom or kitchen should be avoided.

TEMPERATURE

This kind of plant thrives in a warm environment. It'll handle the hottest rooms in your house with ease. On the other hand, if exposed to frosts or near sub-zero temperatures, they will actually fall apart and transform to mush overnight. To be healthy, we recommend never allowing the temperature to drop below 41 °F (5°C).

REPOTTING AND SOIL

The Echeveria has a tendency to stretch out by producing offsets along the edges of the main plant. The adult plant can seldom outgrow its current container (unless you're beginning with a small, fast-growing plant), so if you want it to branch out and generate offsets, you'll need to consider repotting from time to time and make sure the container is larger than the previous one.

They don't require an especially deep container because they don't have a thick root systems. A too deep pot might raise the risk of accidental overwatering and eventual root rot. A shallow and big pot, rather than a deep and narrow one, is your best choice.

KALA CHOE BLOSSFELDIANA

(Flaming Katy)

Flaming Katy, Christmas Kalanchoe, Widow's Thrill, and Florist Kalanchoe are all common names for Kalanchoe Blossfeldiana. It is similar to the jade plant and belongs to the Crassulaceae tribe. Its genus contains over 125 tropical succulent species, the majority of which make excellent indoor plants.

Kalanchoe is a low-cost houseplant that, when in bloom, produces a stunning show of tiny but colorful flowers. The flowers, unfortunately, wilt soon. When this occurs, the plant's only offering is a small bouquet of succulent flowers, which some people may find unappealing.

TRUST ME: ***It only needs to be watered when the soil is completely dry.***

Flaming Katy Care Guide

LIGHT

Kalanchoe can deal with dark places in your home - or workplace - for around one month. This means you can show off their beautiful, yet fleeting, flowers anywhere in your house.

In the long run. low light conditions will cause the plant to become leggy and spindly, destroying the compact structure of this houseplant. They need bright sunshine, preferably an hour or two of direct sunlight every day. If left without light for a prolonged time, it will inevitably die, and the flowers too. The plant can thrive if you choose areas with plenty of light.

WATERING

The Flaming Katy is ideal for the infrequent or forgetful indoor gardener, as it can withstand sporadic and sparse watering thanks to the succulent fleshy leaves' ability to store water for many weeks at a time.

When the soil has dried out somewhat, an attentive owner who wants a healthy plant will water heavily and then wait until it is dry again. This could be once a week during the summer. During the winter months, only a limited amount of water is needed every few weeks at most.

HUMIDITY

The humidity level isn't an issue with this succulent, as it is with many other succulents like houseplants. Even if your home's humidity is high, good ventilation will help avoid basal stem rot and fungus.

REPOTTING

If you decide to maintain the plant after it has stopped flowering, use a soil mix that is either very free draining or apply some grit or sand to the medium you are using while repotting. Repot after a couple of years but be vigilant since the leaves are very fragile and can break quickly if handled roughly.

SPEED OF GROWTH

Regardless of the conditions under which your plant is growing, it will do it slowly. However, since the plant is small to begin with, a little growth over the course of a season will also transform it. Between 3 and 5 years, the optimum height and spread are normally achieved.

HEIGHT / SPREAD

Indoor Kalanchoe rarely grow taller or wider than 12in/ 30cm, making for a delicate specimen. Use a compact vine for best looking results. If your plant gets leggy and spindly, you aren't giving them enough light.

SPATHIPHYLLUM

(Peace Lily)

Peace lilies are evergreen tropical plants that grow in dappled sunshine and consistent rainfall on the forest's floor. The trick to make your peace lily happy and safe is to replicate these circumstances at home. Peace lilies grow white to off-white flowers beginning in early summer and blooming throughout the year if given enough sun.

Peace lilies are a common option for offices and homes. When it comes to indoor plants, peace lily plants are among the simplest to maintain and one of the best to go with modern furniture.

Peace Lily Care Guide

LIGHT

The growth pf your plant would be faster and more vigorous if you place it in a bright spot without direct sunlight. Of course, if you want to cultivate it in a darkened region of your home, it will thrive, adapt, and grow, contrary to popular belief (albeit slowly).

WATERING

Keep the soil just moist at all times. Just keep an eye on the plant for visual cues when it's time to water. When the Lily feels good, you can see it right away, but when it wants water, it flops down. When watering, soak the plant rather than letting it "rest" in water. If you're having trouble with your lily, it's more likely because of how you're watering it.

HUMIDITY

If the humidity in these areas is consistently poor, it can create issues in the long run, so aim to raise the humidity in these areas. Otherwise, a light misting is all that's needed.

REPOTTING

If you do repot, do so in the spring if necessary, this will encourage flowering. You will just need a slightly larger pot and regular houseplant potting mix.

SPEED OF GROWTH

In decent lighting conditions, it will grow moderately. If light levels are low, it will be significantly slower (if at all).

HEIGHT / SPREAD

This is dependent on the kind of fruit you purchase. Even so, in an indoor home environment, they can only hope to grow to a height of 18in / 45cm.

HEDERA HELIX

(English Ivy)

English ivy, also known as Hedera Helix (from Ancient Greek, "twist or turn"), is a simple houseplant to cultivate. Plants of English ivy are evergreen perennials, and Woody vines are another name for them. English ivy should be used as a ground cover because it spreads horizontally and grows to a height of 8 inches. It is, however, a climber, thanks to its aerial rootlets, which allow it to reach heights up to 80 feet. While the plant can eventually produce small greenish flowers, it is mainly cultivated for its evergreen leaves, and in this respect it may be categorized as a foliage plant. Spring is the perfect season to grow English ivy. It's a fast-growing plant, so much that in some areas it is considered invasive.

Since English Ivy is not poisonous, it can be handled like any other herb. Its leaves though, as well as the berries produced by very mature specimens, can be poisonous if consumed.

English Ivy Care Guide

LIGHT

In general, English Ivy comes in variegated or all-green varieties. To keep its colors, the variegated version needs moderate to bright light. The all-green variety will thrive in darker environments, but its development will slow down as a result. However, no direct sunlight is suggested for any kind of ivy.

WATERING

Despite her origins in rainy England, English Ivy despises being soaked or bone dry. You can find a good balance by holding the soil moist. In winter, he soil stays wet for longer stretches of time, so won't need to water as much during the colder seasons.

HUMIDITY

If you want to place the plant in a hot room, you'll need to spray the leaves often, or find other means to keep level of humidity high.

REPOTTING

English Ivy takes a long time to fill a standard sized pot with its roots due to the work it takes to produce aerial roots along its winding stems. When it's time to repot (usually, every 2 to 3 years), you can do so at any time of the year with regular soil or simple potting compost.

SPEED OF GROWTH

Generally the Ivy's growth is quite aggressive. But direct sun will make it grow slower. If on the other hand you can find a comfy shaded spot and use fertilizer to encourage growing, growth can be fast paced, especially for two-year old and more plants.

HEIGHT/SPREAD

A mature Ivy can grow 9 feet per year and its branches will continue to thrive as long as they have enough to cling onto, or as long as you don't pinch out the tops.

JASMINUM POLYANTHUM

(Chinese / Star Jasmine)

Growing vining jasmines as houseplants can be challengeing, but one species that stands out for this purpose is pink jasmine (Jasminum polyathum), also known as white jasmine, Chinese jasmine, or winter-blooming jasmine. White jasmine blooms in late winter, with a profusion of reddish-pink buds that open to reveal star-shaped white flowers tinged with pink. It's rare for houseplants to flower too profusely. Growing jasmine it's ideal for your house if a soft night-time scent, spread by its winter blooms, appeal to your senses.

Although not all jasmine flowers are scented, Jasminum polyanthum, the variety most commonly grown indoors, has a sweet aroma that is especially fragrant at night.

Star Jasmine Care Guide

LIGHT

Both Jasmine plants, whether grown outdoors or indoors, need bright light and, if possible, direct sunlight, so a south-facing window would be ideal for your plant.

WATERING

A Jasmine would need a lot of water when it is in bloom and growing. When in bloom it's very important to remember that the soil must be kept moist nearly all the time. If the soil dries up, the flowers and buds that are about to bloom will wither. Always remember though that with the term "moist" I don't mean soggy or for the plant to sit in a tray of water, that is more on the "wet" side, not "moist", they're not equivalent.

REPOTTING

You're going to need to repot when the Jasmine outgrows its pot. Repotting into larger pots on a regular basis encourages growing, so you can only repot when the roots have fully filled the pot. The best time to do this is in the spring or summer but do not do repot when the buds are already growing. The best compost mix is a standard compost mix that drains well.

SPEED OF GROWTH

During the warmer months of the year, the growth rate of Jasmine can best be characterized as robust. Otherwise, the plant will clamber and ascend, resulting in a messy appearance (if you're okay with that, then let it grow freely).

CRASSULA OVATA

(Jade Plant / Money Plant)

The legend says that there is a plant that is able to bring you wealth and prosperity. If you were wondering what is that plant, it's the beautiful jade plant!

The Jade plant is commonly known as the Money Plant, and together with the Pachira Aquatica, is the most popular "lucky charm plants". The Jade Plant is one of the most well-known (and loved) of the various succulent Crassula used as indoor plants.

The Feng Shui money plants' energy comes from their deep roots and vivid energy of the developing young plant. It is said that you should place her somewhere which somehow represent your finances or your bank account for it to work (for example the table or the drawer where you always use to place your wallet).

Jade Plant Care Guide

LIGHT

A location with a lot of natural sunlight doesn't mean that it will not survive in marginally darker environments... actually it can also thrive in a space with no windows but with artificial lighting!

The leaves can turn a dark purple color if the sunlight is too harsh or the plant is not used to it. If this your case, either place it to a slightly darker place or make more light hit the plant gradually, over time. After few weeks, the purple should disappear and return to the familiar lime green.

WATERING

Jade Plants, like most succulents, are tough and adaptable to a range of conditions, but they won't last long if you overwater them all the time. Water thoroughly and wait for the soil to dry before repeating. In the winter, only enough water should be provided to keep the soil moist.

REPOTTING

Several Crassula species, like the Jade, are happy to remain in the same pot and stale soil for years on end. They don't need to be repotted as much, which is a major plus for an house plant. These plants get big and strong!

When repotting, do it in the spring and be extra vigilant about watering before new fresh growth appears. You'll need a compost blend that drains well.

SPEED OF GROWTH

In the early years, you should assume sluggish to moderate development in good light conditions with a consistent watering schedule. After it reaches maturity, its growth will be a bit more lazy.

HEIGHT/SPEED

The Jade Plant is incredible. It will comfortably equal the average human life span and grow up to a height of 12ft / 4m during that period. It can stretch to over 3ft in diameter, so plenty of room is needed if you want it for the long term. If you have a tiny one, though, don't worry; it will take a long time for it to hit these proportions. And who knows, by the time it req-uires more rooms, it might have boosted your bank account, paid off your mortgage, and allowed you to purchase a larger home to accommodate it!

TRUST ME: ***Jewel Orchids are cultivated for their dark foliage rather than their exotic flowers.***

JEWEL ORCHID

(Ludisia Discolour)

Ludisia discolour, also known as the "Jewel Orchid," is a satisfying and simple-to-care-for houseplant. Its deep purple leaves are flecked with pink streaks and have a velvety look, tolerant of lower light and fond of humidity. Tiny white flowers emerge among the leaves in the right circumstances, rendering this plant a treat for a shadier corner.

The Jewel Orchid (Ludisia discolour) is a unique orchid with stunning dark, ovate-shaped leaves with pink veins. Jewel orchids produce whitish flowers on long flower spikes only once a year. Jewel orchids, unlike many other orchid plants, grow in the ground and enjoy the shade. and

Jewel Orchid Care Guide

LIGHT

The Jewel Orchid grows low in the ground in its natural habitat, sometimes in sunny areas. If you want to obtain the best results, place it under direct sunshine in your home or workplace.

North-facing rooms are ideal, but also any other positioning would work as long as the leaves are shielded from any harsh sunshine that might filter in during the day. Do not mistake this for a plant that thrives in the dark; heavy gloom should be avoided almost as well as bright sunshine if you want your plant to thrive.

WATERING

The Jewel Orchid prefers to flourish in mildly moist conditions. It doesn't like bone dry soil, but it also doesn't like dripping wet soil; if its roots are submerged in water, it will quickly perish.

Water the plant thoroughly, and wait until it is completely dried before watering it again. Wait until the top inch is dry before adding more water, as a general rule. You'll need to spray more often if you're using a more porous potting mix than if you're using regular potting soil so it can dry out faster.

HUMIDITY

Humidity is not a big deal if you got the watering conditions just right. If you know you're a slacker when it comes to watering, help your Jewel Orchid out by growing the humidity in theroom. This would provide a little hedge for your plant to compensate for the lack of watering.

For my experience this plant is perfect for flourishing in bottle gardens, but if you want it to bloom, don't bother: the blooms spoil rapidly in the extremely damp conditions created by the bottle where the plant is kept.

FEEDING

Jewel's orchids are not that hungry, and you'll be fine if you just feed your plant a few times per year. It doesn't matter whether you use a specialty orchid feed or anything more generic; it's not picky, and it will work.

REPOTTING

When the pot becomes overcrowded or the plant becomes wobbly and top-heavy, repot it. Since the roots of these orchids stretch out rather than grow tall, they don't need a deep container. Instead, you might use a shallow and big pot.

Unlike certain orchids, you should use regular potting soil, but you must pay attention to the plant's watering needs to prevent overwatering. Normal potting soil is intended to retain water, but if you unintentionally saturate it, the water can remain in the soil for a long time, greatly increasing the risk of rotting.

SPREADH /WIDTH

Since these orchids like to stretch rather than grow tall, they are often larger than they are tall. The flowering stem will almost triple or double the plant's height.

MONSTERA DELICIOSA

(Swiss Cheese Plant)

This one is everybody's favorite. Probably the queen of houseplants! If you're looking for a plant that resembles a modern art masterpiece, well look no further, you've found it. You've probably already seen her on an interior design magazine, or on somebody'd social media feed, but If you have a room corner that needs to be "arted up" a notch, make sure to grab one of those. These tropical plants can grow up to 10 feet tall and have leaves as large as 12 inches in diameter!

The Swiss cheese plant gets its name from its large, heart-shaped leaves that host holes (called "fenestration") as the plant ages, giving it the appearance of Swiss cheese. The "Delicious Monster" is a tropical annual that is commonly cultivated which is native to Central and South America. It's known for being easy to care for and for her climbing qualities, so supplying it with a stake, moss stick, or trellis to cling to will result in some stunning displays (plus, it will produce larger leaves).

Swiss Cheese Plant Care Guide

LIGHT

Because of their tropical roots, Swiss cheese plants thrive in bright, indirect light or partial shade. They're used to grow in the jungle under the shade of big trees, and they can quickly get burned if exposed to too much direct sunlight. If direct sunshine is inevitable, limit their morning sun exposure to only two or three hours.

Swiss cheese plants like their watering to be regular and on the moist side, but not soaked. Although striking the balance can seem quite difficult, you can quickly determine whether your plant requires water by sticking your finger into the soil about an inch deep before watering your Monstera plant; if the soil seems almost dry to the touch, it's time to water.

TEMPERATURE AND HUMIDITY

The most popular Swiss cheese plants are always grown in a conservatory or greenhouse setting, as these deep-jungle plants rely on high humidity, plenty of moisture, and high temperatures. The more closely you can recreate the plant's natural environment, the better. Mist the plant regularly and place it in a well-lit, wet, and humid bathroom or kitchen. Additionally, a humidifier could also be used nearby to keep the air moist. If unavoidable, you can keep the Monstera above 60 degrees Fahrenheit for a short amount of time, but expect it to experience some die-back.

REPOTTING

Shortly after purchase, a young plant in its first container would need to be repotted. Find a pot that is somewhat larger than the old one, and pot it up into its new home using new compost, as with other houseplants. For at least three months, don't feed (with fertilize) freshly repotted plants.

IS THE MONSTERA DELICIOSA TOXIC?

Watch out for your pets: unfortunately, small animals such as dogs and cats may be poisoned by the Swiss cheese plant. The problem stems from the presence of insoluble calcium oxalate crystals in the plant's leaves, stems, and roots. Even though the Swiss cheese plant is rarely lethal, it's still necessary to call a veterinarian or other medical providers if your pet exhibits any unusual symptoms.

PHALAENOPSIS

(Moth Orchid)

Colorful, long-lasting, and easy to cultivate, the moth orchid is the perfect flower.

The Moth Orchid, also known as the Phalaenopsis Orchid or Phal's, is a well-known and quickly recognizable houseplant. They don't need much maintenance and can last for months on end. They've arguably done more than any other genus to increasing orchids' popularity in general.

Orchids of the genus Phalaenopsis are a very satisfying plant for the eye. They're not fussy, and under the right circumstances, they'll put on a show for months.

Moth Orchid Care Guide

LIGHT

Orchids that thrive in bright, indirect light are known as Light Orchids. The best quality of light comes from an east-facing window. Western or southern light is good as long as it's indirect. North-facing windows don't have adequate illumination in most cases.

WATERING

Overwatering rather than underwatering is more likely to consume a moth orchid (Phalaenopsis sp. and its hybrids). Orchids are commonly grown in bark or sphagnum moss, all of which must be left to dry between watering. (Because bark retains less water than moss, orchids planted in it need more frequent watering.) Water the orchid thoroughly until the bark or moss is dried to the touch and the container is lighter (until water comes through the drainage hole in the bottom of your pot). Orchid roots can never be left in stagnant water. Miniature moth orchids, which are relatively new to the market, are cultivated in smaller pots and can dry out more quickly.

REBLOOMING

You should cut off the bloom spike at the base of an orchid until it has finished flowering. Continue to fertilize. Place the pot in clear, bright light. Within a year, the orchid should flower again.

REPOTTING

The orchid may need to be repotted every few years. Since repotting an orchid will stress it and cause it to lose its blooms, do it while it isn't blooming.

CHRYSANTHEMUM MORIFOLIUM

(Pot Mum / Florists Mum)

Tall, elegant flowers crown a mass of dark-green foliage on the Florist Chrysanthemum. This vine, including daisies, sunflowers, and marigolds, belongs to the Asteraceae family.

The name Chrysanthemum comes from the Greek words chryos, which means gold, and anthemom, which means herb. These "golden roses" come in a variety of colors, including pink, black, crimson, burgundy, white, and, of course, golden yellow.

The Pot Mum, also known as the Florist's Mum, is a common houseplant that is often given as a gift at Christmas, Easter, or Mothering Sunday. It is granted to an individual as a sign of motherhood in certain parts of the world, such as shortly after the recipient has given birth.

Pot Mum Care Guide

LIGHT

Bright light is needed in all situations. The weak winter sun, or early morning / late afternoon Summer sun will be most beneficial.

WATERING

Watering the Pot Mum leads to a high transpiration rate, which is one of the reasons it is so good at cleaning the air. For best result, you will need to water it often, perhaps twice a week. Maintain constant moisture in the soil.

HUMIDITY

There is no reason to be careful with humidity if the plant is being used as a temporary pot plant. If you want to keep it for a long time, keep it away from very dry and low-humidity environments.

FEEDING

Any decent all-purpose fertilizer once a month.

REPOTTING

Repotting isn't necessary because it won't be around long enough to outgrow it. The Crysnthemus container it comes in. If you plan on having it, follow standard repotting procedures. i.e., replace the current pot with a slightly larger one.

Flowers are usually the prime justification for purchasing a plant in the first place. While the doubles look good with their upbeat cheerleader pompon like appearance, the single flowers with the daisy like yellow centers are the most common. Except for blue and black, they are available in any color hue.

EFFICIENT AIR CLEANERS

Beautiful florist chrysanthemums work hard at reducing air pollution present in homes caused by contaminants in upholstery, paint, and carpet, including being transient houseguests. "Florist mums are one of the safest flowering plants for removing formaldehyde, benzene, and ammonia from indoor air".

EPIPREMNUM AUREUM

(Pothos / Devil's Ivy / Scindapsus)

Pothos, one of the most popular plant in the houseplant realm. Also known as Devil's Ivy, is a low-maintenance houseplant that is almost foolproof to cultivate indoors. It can be seen in people's houses, offices, and even shopping malls. When you start to notice, it's everywhere!

Because of its beautiful light lime-colored leaves with yellow variegation, golden pothos is one of the most common varieties of hanging basket plants. The lemon-colored brush strokes on its leaves together with their sinuous shapes makes it also very elegant. The pothos helps br shaded corners with its shiny leaves.

The golden pothos is an exceptional low-light herb, which is one (notable characteristics. Plants with variegated leaves typically vibrancy when exposed to low light; the golden pothos, on the ot keeps its vivid variegation even in low light. Because of this, gold is a good choice for a bedroom plant with access to minimal ligh

TRUST ME: ***These vines are very easy to care for and can gr a variety of lighting and watering conditions.***

Pothos Care Guide

LIGHT

If you chose a very dark place, growth will be gradual, and the "vines" will be thin, with leaves spaced far apart. Very bright patches of direct sunshine on the leaves should also be avoided, as this would inevitably kill the plant. If the room is so bright that you have to squint your eyes to be able to read a book, it is probably a room where your Pothos would be unhappy to live. Despite their hardiness, too much sun will cause their leaves to yellow and 'burn,' so keep them away from the windowsill.

WATERING

Areate the soil in your pot if you have a new plant. Before watering check there is no moist 1 inch under the soil's surface. During winters water more sparingly. The Pothos is drought tolerant, so your plant won't mind too much if sometimes you delay the watering. Overwatering, on the other

hand, must be prevented at all costs, or rot will develop around the roots. It is never a good idea to have soggy or muddy soil. Pour some extra water away if you've supplied too many.

A decent soak once a week is probably best. Many factors, however are in play: plants in warm rooms with loads of light require more water than those in colder spots with less light.

REPOTTING

It will take some years for the Pothos to need repotting. The most noticeable indication that it's time for a repot is when it is no longer expanding in sum mer time (growth shouldn't be expected in the winter).

Pothos like to stretch their muscles out as well. If your vines get long and twisted, gently hang their branches on a few tacked pins around their growing space and you'll have lovely vines growing around your walls in no time.

OXALIS

(Purple Shamrock / False or Love Plant)

This one will probably not appeal everybody, but I find its beauty one of the most fascinating plant that can be kept inside our house. Get one of this and you can be consider a houseplant pro.

With its purple foliage - sometimes nearly black - the Purple shamrock (Oxalis triangularis), also known as false shamrock, will unavoidably draw the interest of the whole room they're placed in. Its deep purple leaves are triangular in shape and usually emerge in threes. The way the leaves of these plants close at night is a curious touch. In the evening, the leaves fold down like an umbrella, and remain closed during the night (or on especially cloudy days), but they open up again with the morning sun.
Other rare responsive houseplants have identical movements (Mimosa pudica).

The plant produces tiny flowers that range in color from white to pale pink or lavender. Purple shamrock thrives as a houseplant and is better grown in the spring.

Purple Shamrock Care Guide

LIGHT

This plant thrives under a wide range of conditions, from full sun to partial shade. If you're raising it outside in a hot environment, give it some shade from the sun during the afternoon. The plant should be grown near a window that receives plenty of light. Rotate the pot on a regular basis to ensure that both sides of the plant are exposed to light and are rising uniformly. The plant will become sluggish and leggy if it receives insufficient light.

SOIL

Purple shamrocks can thrive in a variety of soil types as long as they have adequate drainage. If the soil absorbs so much moisture, the roots are vulnerable to rotting. The perfect soil is loamy or sandy. A general, well-draining potting mix should suffice for container development.

WATERING

Water to ensure an even amount of soil moisture, especially for young purple shamrock plants. More mature plants are drought tolerant and will forgive the occasionale lack of watering. Feed purple shamrock plants once the top inch of soil has dried out during the growing season. In the summer, when the plant is dormant, water it gently every two to three weeks to keep the soil from drying out entirely.

TEMPERATURE AND HUMIDITY

These plants prefer temperatures between 60 to 75 degrees Fahrenheit, making them ideal for growing indoors in typical room temperatures. They can withstand temperatures as low as 50 degrees Fahrenheit at night. Protect the plants from strong winds, including those from air conditioners and heaters, which can harm the foliage. Purple shamrock plants thrive in a moderately humid environment.

FERTILIZER

During the growing season, fertilize the purple shamrock plant with a slow-release or liquid fertilizer. A liquid fertilizer for houseplants is suitable for indoors use. Incorporating compost into the soil will also aid in the promotion of healthy development.

IS THE PURPLE SHAMROCK TOXIC?

When swallowed, oxalis plants are poisonous to both humans and animals. Both areas of the plant are toxic, with the bulbs having the largest concentration of toxins.

CHLOROPHYTUM

(Spider Plant)

Spider plants (or Chlorophytum comosum) have a rosette of long, thin, arched foliage that is either solid green or white variegated. These houseplants are particularly attractive in a hanging basket and were common in Victorian-era homes.

TRUST ME: ***When the flowers fade, tiny plantlets appear in their place, eventually growing their own seeds.***

Spider plants are among the most common houseplants to cultivate, despite their creepy-crawly name. They can thrive in less-than-ideal environments, and they look beautiful when grown in a tropical environment. The leaves of these plants are slender and softly arching, ranging in length from 1 to 1.5 feet on average. The leaves may be grey or green and white striped. Long stems with tiny star-shaped flowers are frequently sent out by mature plants.

Spider Plant Care Guide

LIGHT

To retain their stripes, all variegated Spider Plants need a bright spot. The all-green version (which has no variegation to lose) can evolve in a darker setting, but at a much slower rate. Direct sunlight should be avoided at all costs.

WATERING

In the growing months (Spring to Autumn/Fall), water your plant thoroughly, and if you've placed it in a bright spot, you'll see rapid growth and a fair chance of Spider babies. Water sparingly in the winter because growth slows down regardless of what you do, and too much water sloshing around the roots will cause the plant to rot.

REPOTTING

If given proper care, a Spider Plant would need to be repotted into a larger pot every Spring before it reaches maturity, which takes around 2 to 5 years. You may use standard houseplant or garden compost for this. If you're concerned that your plant is already too big and you won't be able to move it, don't repot it into a larger jar, as this will limit its growth.

HOYA KERRII

(Sweetheart Plant / Valentine Hoya)

There are a few Hoya species that make excellent houseplants, one of which is Hoya kerrii, also known as the Sweetheart Vine. While it has grown in popularity in recent years, you might still have trouble finding facts or care tips regarding this plant. If you think the leaves of Hoya kerrii are the cutest thing about it, just wait after it blooms. The flowers have a strong scent, making them a good source of perfume fragrances.

Hoya Kerrii Care Guide

LIGHT

This plant would need a moderate amount of light to thrive, but it will survive in a shadier area too. However, very dark areas should be avoided. Sunlight is also appropriate, because it may be placed virtually anywhere in your home or workplace.

WATERING

The Hoya can store water for long stretches of time between waterings thanks to its succulent qualities. For the most part, this makes it a hardy and low-maintenance plant; however, if this is the only treatment you will be willing to give her, do not expect much love back. Water it regularly when the soil has dried out and you can hope for them to reward you with one of the most beautiful and peculiar flower houseplants could give you. As always, be careful not to go overboard! The soil should never be wet or flooded, since this would bring rot. Take extra precautions, especially if the pot you're using doesn't have any drainage holes.

FEEDING

Because the plant only has one leaf, only a small amount of fertilizer is needed, twice a year. You can feed it a little more if you have an older plant or if the single leaf is producing new shoots. If that's the case, I suggest to not doing it more than four times a year.

REPOTTING

This topic is a source of controversy among Hoya owners. There are many schools of thinking that can be boiled down to the following "rules":

• The soil mix must drain well and not have a lot of rich organic matter.

• Plants that are root or pot attached in small containers are more likely to bloom (this only applies to mature plants with many leaves).

• No matter how big or old the plant is, if the pot is too little, it will not mature.

• A large pot for plants with just one leaf has a much higher chance of rotting due to unintended overwatering (so don't do it).

So, to put it all into perspective, here are few explanations that should make sense:

• Young plants with only one leaf can be repotted only as new growth appears.

- Young plants with a few leaves can be repotted every couple of years, each time going up into a much larger tank.
- Mature plants with several leaves can be repotted every couple of years at the maximum, each time going up into a slightly larger container.

TILLANDSIA

(Blue Flowered Torch)

Tillandsia cyanea, or Pink Quill Plant, is a lovely little plant. This plant is one of the most common and simplest to grow bromeliads, and it can be used as a small container plant, hanging basket, or epiphyte attached to wood.

The blue-flowered torch is a perennial herb that grows on a variety of plants. It has 30 to 50 cm rosettes of arching dark green leaves. Green to purple-pink floral bracts and funnel-shaped, scented white-eyed, deep purple-blue flowers with spreading petals are produced by this herb. The flower-flowering stem is a plump blade-like feather that can reach 7,8 inches in length and is made up of thick, flattened pink bracts from which the large, bluish flowers emerge, often referred to by bromeliad collectors as a "paddle-shaped inflorescence."

Tillandsa Care Guide

LIGHT

The perfect light for your Pink Quill Plant is clear, natural light. That's where an east or west exposure comes in handy. You want it in this light to encourage flowering and keep the plant satisfied over time. Do not put the Tillandsia under direct sunlight, not the right kind of light for this little tender beauty.

WATERING

Very low effort is needed to maintain the Tillandsia in good shape. Water it once or max twice a week, depending on how dusty the conditions are.

Water less in the late fall/winter months, as with all houseplants. If the water is rough, use purified or distilled water instead, as this plant is sensitive to mineral build-up in tap water. Some prefer to use tap water that has sat long enough for the chlorine contained to dissipate. Try and see to what kind of water your plant react better.

FERTILIZING

I rarely fertilize my bromeliads or air plants; only once a year if they seem to need it. This plant gets its moisture and nutrients from the leaves rather than the soil, for this reason, it's best to spray the fertilizer onto the foliage & the surface of the growing medium.

You may use this fertilizer designed for air plants or an all-purpose orchid food diluted to 1/2 strength. You can fertilize in the spring and/or summer, and it should be done once or twice a year.

REPOTTING

If you buy a Tillandsia that is already in bloom, there is no need to repot it. Repot and upsize the pot next spring if the roots have filled the pot and/or you see a young offset.

Don't worry if this doesn't happen because the Pink Quill plant's roots are simple and compact. It's important to always be aware if there is at least a tiny amount of room for new roots to expand through. The potting mix you select must be free drainage, which means regular potting compost combined with a little grit or perlite would suffice.

AECHMEA FASCIATA

(Urn Plant / Silver Vase plant)

Aechmea fasciata is a flowering bromeliad plant that can be cultivated both indoors and outdoors, depending on the environment. The Urn plant has a completely different impact if you observe it from far rather than you do it by a closer inspection.

The urn bulb is one the most common Aechmea genus bromeliad for growing and displaying indoors. The traditional name come from the fact that the plant's core resembles an urn or vase. This vase form captures water in its natural environment, and the grower should fill it as much as nature expected. After a couple of years of maturity, this plant develops a large flower head that can last from mid-summer to early winter.

When an Aechmea Fasciata reaches maturity (after a few years), it produces a bract that becomes bright pink over time. It has a long flowering cycle, and these plants truly reward their owners with the familiar, long-lasting inflorescence during this time.

Urn Plant Care Guide

LIGHT

The majority of Bromeliads are epiphytic, meaning they grow on larger plants such as trees. Visualize a plant catching on a tree trunk so you can imagine how it will flourish in its natural habitat. In this environment, her natural home is below the canopy and away from the harsh direct light, away from the very dark sunny spots at the base of the tree.

When growing these plants in our homes, attempt to provide bright indirect light to imitate their preferred light conditions. It can also thrive in light shade but avoid heavy shade or rooms with no curtains.

If you want to get the plant to flowering level, you'll need more sun. Avoid direct sunshine at all costs, or you risk scorching the leaves and forever destroying the plant's aspect.

WATERING

Aechmea are opportunistic plants in their natural habitat, collecting water in their central "vase" or "urns." The flower bract arises from the vase, which is the central container.They don't have a large root system, but the majority of their irrigation needs are fulfilled by the water contained in their urns. Since these houseplants aren't big drinkers, don't overwater them at any point. Keep the central vase full, emptying and refilling it once a month to keep the liquid from being stagnant.

If the vase is full, you just need to water the compost until it dries out entirely. This will most likely happen every few weeks. And even more so in very hot weather. If you don't want to water with a vase, try to keep the soil partially damp at all times.

TEMPERATURE

If given the choice, all Aechmea would prefer warmer temperatures. However, they aren't too concerned about temperature in general. Temperatures range from 59°F (15°C) to 77°F (25°C).

TRADESCANTIA ZEBRINA

(Wandering Jew Plant / Inch Plant)

The Wandering Jew, also known as the Inch Rose, Spiderwort, or Tradescantia Zebrina, is a houseplant that can be grown in a hanging basket to display its long trailing vines or kept enclosed and compact in a pot. This plant is very flexible, quick to grow, and difficult to destroy, making it an excellent indoor plant to have around.

As a hanging or trailing indoor vine, Tradescantia zebrina is valued for its ease of care and colorful foliage of silver, purple, and green that brightens up any room.

TRUST ME: ***Wandering Jew (or, more recently, Wandering Dude) gets its name from its ability to effectively root and survive in a variety of environments.***

Wandering Jew Plant Care Guide

LIGHT

The variegated colors on the leaves of all Tradescantias, including the Wandering Jew Plants, require a lot of light to stay vibrant; if the light is too dark, the colors will fade.

In the other hand, if it is exposed to too much illumination, leaf scorching occurs; luckily, however, the phenomenon of "too much light" is mostly exacerbated by overly exposed areas during the season. This is difficult to do indoors, so you'll only be at risk if you let your plants outside in Summer.

WATERING

As you'd imagine from any hardy houseplant, the Wandering Jew can handle droughts and a little water logging now and again.

However, if that's how you water your plants you should stop this sloppy watering technique as soon as possible: if you want a good-looking plant, it needs to be properly watered. The method is simple: water your Tradescantia often and liberally during the summer months to keep the soil moist for as long as possible. In the winter, cut back sharply so development can stall or cease entirely, reducing the need for water drastically.

REPOTTING

It's best to repot once a year to allow the roots a little more room to flourish, but this plant, like many houseplant, will survive growing in the same soil for years. This is especially useful if you've wanted to grow it in a hanging basket, which can be fiddly to upsize and difficult to deal with.

When you do need to repot, regular potting soil is a perfect option; just quit the mixes with a lot of manure and don't use ordinary dirt from your yard.

ZAMIOCULCAS ZAMIIFOLIA

(ZZ Plant)

Zamioculcas zamiifolia, also known as the ZZ plant, is a tropical perennial native to Eastern Africa that has gained worldwide popularity in recent years due to its adaptability to a variety of conditions. The soft, naturally glossy leaves of the ZZ vary in color from light lime in youth, to emerald green in maturity.

With its large, beautiful, dark green leaves, the ZZ plant has a lot of advantages for offices and homes. The ZZ plant is tolerant of neglect, drought, and low light levels without being too much irritated. The waxy leaves reflect light and can brighten rooms. ZZ grows slowly to a height and width of two to three feet, which means this isn't a monster plant that easily outgrows containers.

The ZZ Plant has a number of advantages, including being trendy, beautiful, and easy to care for, as well as having a simple propagation process.

ZZ Plant Care Guide

LIGHT

This plant thrives in medium to poor indirect sunlight. Allows for bright indirect light to be used. Intense, direct sunlight is not recommended.

Early morning or late afternoon sun is preferable, so choose a window that faces north, east, or west. If you want it to flourish, you should also keep it out of deep shade.

WATERING

Enable 2-3 weeks between waterings to allow the soil to dry out. Watering should be done more often in higher light and less often in lower light.

Since the plant is adapted to surviving droughts, frequent watering without allowing the soil to dry between applications will make the leaves yellow before rotting the tubers.

The soil, on the other hand, needs to be damp for the majority of the time between late Spring and early Autumn / Fall for productive and rapid development.

HUMIDITY

Average home humidity is fine; dry air can be tolerated.

TEMPERATURE

Temperatures range from 60°F to 85°F. The average temperature of our houses will most likely make the ZZ's life more than comfortable.

SIZE

The ZZ may grow slowly, but at the peak of its growth it can reach a height between 16″ to 28″.

IS THE ZAMIOCULCAS ZAMIIFOLIA TOXIC?

Yes, when swallowed, it is poisonous. But by now you should have realized that houseplants should be kept out of sight of young children and pets anyway.

CYCLAMEN PERSICUM

(Cyclamen)

Cyclamen (Cyclamen persicum) is a compact flowering plant with sweet-scented, small (1/2- to 3/4-inch) blooms on long stems rising above the foliage. The Cyclamen is a tuberous annual, which means it dies down to its dense roots (tubers) in the summer and regrows easily in the fall. Its flowers are pink, yellow, red, and white in color. It also has medium-green heart-shaped leaves with silver marbling.

It's widely grown as a houseplant, and it's especially popular during the holidays, when you can find cyclamen blooming on store shelves.
Indoors, cyclamens are normally cultivated in pots. They go dormant during the summer, but given a decent treatment, it can rebloom in the fall.

TRUST ME: ***The timing of cyclamen's full dormancy is determined by its rising conditions.***

Cyclamen Care Guide

SOIL

Cyclamen favors a mildly acidic soil pH and organically rich, well-draining soil. You may use standard potting mix for container plants but add some sphagnum peat to the soil to increase the acidity.

WATERING

The presence of leaves indicates that the plant is actively growing. Water if the soil feels dry about an inch below the surface. Water should not be applied to the plant's leaves or crown (the area where the stem joins the roots), since this will most likely cause it to rot. Water infrequently when the plant is inactive (losing any or more of its leaves), just enough to keep the soil from drying out completely.

TEMPERATURE AND HUMIDITY

Cyclamen plants dislike high temperatures, draughts, and dry air. They thrive in a climate that is similar to their natural habitat, with temperatures ranging from 40 to 50 degrees Fahrenheit at night and 60 to 70 degrees Fahrenheit during the day. The importance of high humidity, particularly in the winter, cannot be overstated. Hold the plant on a tray filled with water and pebbles to increase humidity, just make sure the pot is not in contact with the water (as this could cause root rot).

Usually this plant stays outside; if you do bring your plant back inside if the weather gets cold. A safe rule of thumb is to put it indoors when the weather is already pleasant enough to open the curtains.

FERTILIZER

When in full leaf, feed your cyclamen plant with a diluted liquid low-nitrogen fertilizer every couple of weeks.

CHAPTER
3
The World of Succulent

WHAT ARE SUCCULENT PLANTS?

Succulents are water-storing plants with fleshy, thickened leaves and/or bloated roots. The word "succulent" is derived from the Latin word sucus, which means "juice or sap". Succulents are very drought resistant and they can thrive on small water supply such as dew and mist. For this reason they are ideal for new aspiring houseplant growers.

Succulents come in a wide variety of varieties and cultivars, spanning many plant families, but most people equate succulents with the cactus genus, Cactaceae. (Keep in mind, however, that although cacti are succulents, succulents are not all cacti).

Based on personal experience, my suggestion is: never underestimated the power of a succulent in a living room. They've been used in interior decor magazines, and on social media, as part of lavish wedding centrepieces, but also in minimalistic environments, where they give the focal point that enriches the room.

Right now, succulents are quite the trend. The oft-repeated assertion that succulents are simple to grow is only partially true. I'm going to give you some guidelines to follow if you want to successfully host succulents or cacti in your home.

Having said that, if you mess this up, you're good at messing things up.

WHAT SUCCULENTS NEED:

1. The right amount of light

The most complex environmental element to replicate indoors is the ambient light in a plant's native habitat. This aspect is easier to deal with when growing traditional houseplants. Many of them are used to the alternating cycles of shade and sun that occur in your household, having grown up in tropical jungles. After all, that's what happens as the sun rays pass through a tree canopy.

You're begging for disappointment if you put a plant that's used to being out in the scorching sun for a full 12 hours on an east-facing sill.

Choose the sunniest south-facing window you can find, and if none of your windows face south, go with a more tolerant succulent like aloe or give up and go get a sturdy Pothos.

2. The right amount of water

The Chihuahuan Desert receives just over 9 inches of rain a year, a drop in the bucket as opposed to the lush deserts that most of us call home. When it rains in the desert, though, it pours. To keep your desert-dwelling pet comfortable, attempt to imitate the rain patterns seen in its natural environment. Turn on the taps and let loose a deluge on your cacti instead of a trickle.Succulents (and all plants, for that matter) profit from a thorough soaking, which can last until the water runs out from the bottom of the container. Wait until the soil is fully dried before watering succulents again. Succulent's dislike sitting in wet dirt, so irrigation is important to avoid rot. A drainage hole should be present in your container to allow excess water to drain. Beginners can use terra-cotta pots.

3. The right Potting Soil

From ferns to fiddle-leaf figs, most potted plants come in a standard soil mix that fits with almost any kind of plant. The issue: succulents are designed to survive one of the harshest conditions on the planet, so regular potting soil won't suffice.

Adjust the soil in your succulent baby's home to a desert-dweller blend, which consists of half potting soil and something inorganic like perlite. Most succulents can thrive in this super well-draining, low-nutrient soil, whether they're used to thriving in the high and dry Andes or the scorching bottom lands of Death Valley.

4. The right amount of space

One big blunder is overcrowding succulents. Succulents are always packaged in cute little bowls, stuffed cheek to jowl. This set up is not the best idea though, as they are among the plants that don't like this setup. It is actually one of the most effective ways to promote mold and insect infestations.

The second problem is that, while succulents can survive on very little, they do need food and water. It is possible they start to suffer if there's so much competition. If your succulents arrive in a crowded arrangement, carefully separate them and give each one its own mini desert dune.

5. Grow the right Types

I know it's difficult to fight the temptation to cultivate saguaros (your typical desert cactus) indoors, but please don't. Some wild things, no matter how lovely their flowers or alluring their shape, are simply not meant to be tamed. Instead, go for the tough little cookies that will gladly embrace the windowsill as their forever home.

If you're dealing in indoor environments, Crassula and Sansevieria (a.k.a. snake plant) are fine choices. If you're searching for a prickly plant friend, the Mammillaria cacti (named after their woolly hair) is a fine option.

6. Get Rid of Bugs

Indoor succulents may be pest-free, but you will have to deal with pests on occasion. Gnats are drawn to succulents that have been planted in wet soils with poor drainage. Spray the soil with 70% isopropyl alcohol to get rid of eggs and larvae. Another insect that succulent owners must contend with is mealybugs. Mealybugs are commonly caused by overwatering and overfertilizing. Spray contaminated plants with 70% isopropyl alcohol and move them away from other succulents.

IDENTIFYING YOUR SUCCULENT PLANT

Succulents are a wide group that contains thousands of plants, both indoor and outdoor, making it impossible to classify a single genus and species. Succulent plants have several generic names that can be used interchangeably, making identification difficult. A individual may take a few steps to get a correct identification, which mostly rely on using the plant's physical characteristics as descriptors.

The Identification Process

Simply ask the plant seller which succulent plant is being purchased to prevent a lengthy identifying procedure. If the seller does not know or it is not practicable to inquire, begin by determining if the plant is a succulent or a cactus, and then narrowing down the species by examining the plant's leaf form and overall structure.First of all to differentiate a succulent from a cactus. Cactus plants generally have few or no leaves. We can recognize them thanks to the indentations, or areoles, along heir stems, from which the traditional spines spring.

Leaf Shape

From the large, thin, triangle-shaped leaves of an Aloe vera plant to the short, almost perfectly spherical leaves of a Senecio rowleyanus, also known as String of Pearls, succulents may have a wide range of leaf shapes. Knowing the leaf shape alone sometimes will help identify succulents quickly, especially in the case of succulents with very unusual leaf shapes, such as the String of Pearls.

Rosette Shape

The rosette form of succulent plants is characterized by tight clusters of leaves radiating out from a central point, almost like a rose. The leaves of some rosette succulents are pointed, while the leaves of others are rounded. I invite you to explore many of them, if you just stop and observe the many Echeverias in the market, you may be surprised of how much many of them look like beautiful mandalas.

Overall Configuration and Age

Succulents may have long stalks or strands, or they can be squat and close to the ground, rising outwards rather than upwards. Some succulents begin as a cluster of leaves poking out of the soil and develop into a tall, treelike structure with woody stems and leaves only on the plant's outermost parts, while others begin as a cluster of leaves poking out of the soil and grow into a tall, treelike structure with woody stems and leaves only on the plant's outermost parts. As a result, certain succulents can become easier to recognize as they develop and mature.

Plant Size

The average size of a plant will also aid in identification. Succulents that are either 2.8 to 3.1 inches (7 or 8 centimeters) tall or high are usually grown indoors, while bigger succulents are usually grown in a greenhouse. Plant size descriptors may assist a succulent owner in narrowing down their options.

Flower Color and Shape

If the succulent has distinguishing flowers, this detail may be helpful in determining its identity. The season in which the succulent blooms is also significant. Christmas cacti, for example, have long, colorful flowers with petals that bloom in early to mid-winter, typically just before Christmas, hence the term ***"Christmas Cactus."***

Other Significant Details

There are a few other specifics that will assist in the detection of a succulent plant. If the plant has some easily described physical characteristics, such terms will serve as the plant's identification keywords. You most certainly have a Haworthiopsis attenuata or Haworthiopsis fasciata if you have a succulent with green, spiky leaves with white stripes. A plant owner can have a Sedum morganianum, also known as a Burro's Tail or Donkey's Tail, if the succulent plant has long, overlaying beanie leaves.

BEST INDOOR SUCCULENTS FOR YOUR HOUSE

In most cases, succulents make excellent indoor plants. They're low-maintenance, and since they're indigenous to sunny, dry climates, they're tolerant of a certain level of neglect. Echeveria or Jade plants are common choices for indoor succulent collections. They're like the entrance to the succulent kingdom. You'll certainly want to broaden your succulent horizons after you've had those for a while and maybe even propagated a few leaves here and there.

You will have the chance to select from a variety of exotic and unusual-looking succulent varieties. There are a plethora of eye-catching varieties to choose from, as well as strange and wonderful new leaves to begin your collection.

I already suggested you few succulents that areas to take care for in the above pages. I would like here to suggest you some very peculiar specimen, that would make you love this plants and will take your green passion to another level.

GENERAL SUCCULENT CARE

Let's start with some simple succulent care tips before we get into the unusual succulents I will be suggesting you. There are few general instructions for caring for succulents. Do however your due diligence on individual succulents to see if they need any special treatment.

- ***Succulents Need Sunlight***: Most succulents prefer a hot, dry, and sunny environment in which to grow. Place the plant in a brightly lit area of your house. Choose the windowsill with the most sunlight. If you don't have enough natural light for your succulents, they can spread out in an attempt to reach the light. If this occurs, either bring the plant closer to the window or invest in a plant grow lamp. These lamps don't have to be costly and will provide enough light for your plant.
- ***Succulents Don't Need So Much Water***: Succulents aren't used to a lot of rain and they're from hot climates. As a result, don't overwater your farm. You don't want succulents to sit in moist soil for too long and they're accustomed to dry conditions. Before watering, make sure the soil is fully dry. In the winter, use even less water. Succulents retain water in their leaves, allowing them to withstand drought.
- ***Succulents Need Proper Drainage***: Succulents Need Proper Drainage: Choose a pot with drainage holes in the rim. This allows any extra water to drain after you've watered your succulent. Often, use cactus and succulent soil that drains well. You don't want the soil to be soggy. The roots thrive once the soil is well-drained.

FRITHIA PULCHRA

(Friry Elephant Feet)

Frithia pulchra succulents are called "fairy elephant's feet" for a reason: their green leaves with translucent tips resemble tiny elephant feet. Frithia pulchra, like baby toes succulents, is a window succulent that has adapted well to the harsh grasslands it grows in.

It's not the easiest succulent to produce, but if you follow the instructions carefully, you shouldn't have any trouble keeping it alive.

Frithia pulchra has adapted to spend the most of its time partially underground in order to flourish in this harsh environment. The transparent leaf tips are often the only parts of the plant that are visible.

TRUST ME: ***They encourage light to penetrate deep into the leaf's sections that aren't exposed to direct sunlight.***

Friry Elephant Feet Care Guide

LIGHT

The natural habitat of this succulent is very sunny. It will possibly take every light you give it in your house. Also direct sunlight should not be an issue, but you will need to dig the plant a little deeper into the substrate to prevent scorching..

TEMPERATURE

Frithia pulchra can withstand a wide range of temperatures, as one might imagine from such a hardy little succulent. In reality, if it's buried deep enough in the substrate so that only its leaf tips protrude, it should be able to withstand even the hottest summers.

The cold winters aren't a problem either. And light frost won't damage the plants as long as the soil is kept totally dry.

SENECIO BARBARTONICUS

(Himalaya)

Senecio Barbertonicus is a flowering succulent genus belonging to the Asteraceae family. Succulent Bush Senecio, Finger-leaved Senecio, Lemon Bean Bush, and Barberton Groundsel are all names for Senecio Barbertonicus.

Senecio barbertonicus Himalaya is a plant with densely packed, long, needle-like, bright green leaves and fragrant clusters of yellow tubular flowers. In urban interiors, these charming, spreading succulents add a touch of fun and texture. In the spring, expect little sparky yellow flowers.

Senecio Himalaya Care Guide

The succulent "Succulent Bush" is ideal for bringing variety and texture to container gardens and arrangements. Because of its height, this "Succulent Bush" will become heavy and tip over. Behead the top as it starts to flop until the stem is solid again.

LIGHT

From full light to partial light shade, the Barbertonicus will stay strong, until the light is bright and indirect. If you have the option to choose, a little early morning or late afternoon sun would work.

WATERING

Senecio is a drought-tolerant plant that stores water in its leaves. Allow the soil to dry out between waterings, yet do not overwater the plants or make them sit in water.

TEMPERATURE

Optimal room temperatures are 64 to 75F (18-24°C); but, when the plant is dormant during the winter, Senecio can withstand colder temperatures as low as 50F (10°C).

HEIGHT AND GROWTH

7-8 in (20-25cm) is the maximum height this plant can reach, and it will get taller slowly. Over the summer, apply a balanced fertilizer once a month.

CRASSULA RUPESTRIS MARNERIANA

Crassula Rupestris Marnieriana (or Hottentot) is a species of Crassula Rupestris. The Crassula plant family is likely familiar to succulent enthusiasts. Many of them are noteworthy for their peculiar leaf stacking and odd shapes. With clustered leaves arranged perfectly one on top of the other,

Crassula worm plants exemplify the fantastical arrangement of a living necklace.

TRUST ME: ***The 'Hottentot' is a perfect little addition to any creepy and quirky set.***

Crassula Rupestris Care Guide

LIGHT

In their natural environment, they prefer direct sunshine all day, but as a house plant, they prefer bright but indirect light, rarely lying in direct morning or afternoon sunlight, trying to completely avoid direct sunlight during the midday sun. Exposed to direct sunlight, they will likely burn.

WATERING

Their succulent nature ensures the retention of water in its fleshy leaves, needing very little watering. When the soil is totally dry to the touch, water the vine. The easiest way to water it, is to hold the plant in its pot under flowing water while being careful not to get some water on the leaves themselves. Hold the pot over the sink and let the water soak into it until it no longer drips. After that, you should return it to its original location.

POTTING

Place your Crassula in a pot with plenty of drainage holes. Only the most seasoned succulent growers should attempt to plant them in a dish without a drainage hole, as overwatering or leaving them in moist conditions is the easiest way to destroy them. The roots will decay, and the plant will die as a result.

You won't need to water the plant again for another 2-3 weeks, maybe longer, based on the humidity level in your household. Regularly inspect the soil and then water the plant if the soil is totally dry to the touch.

The Crassula can be held in the same pot for many years. If it outgrows its container, replace it with a cactus and succulent compost that drains well and has a drainage medium like perlite.

GROWTH AND FLOWERING

In the spring and summer, this Crassula may produce a large number of small white or pink flowers.

FERTILIZER

From April to September, apply a succulent fertilizer 4-6 times.

XEROSICYOS DANGUYI

(Silver Dollar Plant)

Xerosicyos danguyi, also known as "Silver Dollar Plant," "Dollar Vine," or "Penny Plant," is a unique climbing succulent vine with dense, succulent, round silvery-green leaves and cylindrical roots. Climbing tendrils are found opposite the leaves, which are 1 to 2 inches long and thick.

Silver dollar vine, despite its appearance, belongs to the Cucurbitaceae family, which includes cucumbers. When the plant starts throwing out curly tendrils to catch and crawl with, you'll see the similarity. This means it begins its life on the ground and quickly scales higher objects, such as trees, in search of light. It may also become a pest, overtaking trees and making it difficult for them to grow fruit or even survive. On the other hand, Danguyi does not grow to be nearly as large or offensive as an indoor hoseplant.

Silver Dollar Plant Care Guide

WATERING

The Silver dollar is drought resistant. Actually when aggressively rising, Xerosicyos danguyi may take in more water. In cold weather, keep the soil drier to prevent root rot, just watering sufficiently to keep the leaves from shriveling.

USES

This is a unique succulent vine that scrambles up and hides fences, walls, and other obstacles. It may also be stored indoors in bright light as a hanging basket or container plant.

PROPAGATION

Soft wood cuttings can be used to propagate this plant by allowing them to callus over and then potting them up. It's even possible to grow it from seed. At 70°F (21°C), seeds germinate in 14-21 days. Plants that are cultivated from seed will form a caudex, but cuttings will not.

CRASSULA

(Buddha's Temple)

This is a special Crassula that I highly recommend. Also known as Buddha's Temple, it's a tall upright succulent with 'stacked' leaves columns that look like a Buddhist pagoda. At the top of each column, mature happy plants bear pompoms of pink flowers.

This Crassula succulent has a perfectly symmetrical tower appearance that would impress even the most pretentious succulent aficionado, making it look like a Buddhist shrine. Crassula CV. is a living sculpture that is also very easy to develop and care for.

Crassula Care Guide

LIGHT

The light Crassula plants prefer full sun over partial shade. During the hottest part of the day, however, the strong afternoon sun will burn the plants' leaves. If provided enough light, most Crassulas can be grown indoors.

TEMPERATUR

Crassula 'Buddha's Temple' can tolerate temperatures as low as 25 to 50 °F (-3.9 to 10 °C).

WATERING

Crassula plants need the same amount of water as other succulents. Overwatering can be avoided by using the "soak and dry" process, which involves soaking the soil in water, steadily draining it, and then allowing it to dry before watering again. In the winter, watering can be reduced.

Buddha's Temple Crassulas don't mind if the soil is acidic or alkaline, but they do like a porous, well-drained soil.

FERTILIZING

When Crassulas begin vigorously growing in mid-spring, they may benefit from a limited amount of organic fertilizer.

REPOTTING & PROPAGATION

Repot if required, preferably in the spring, at the start of an active growth cycle. Crassulas are usually propagated from stem or leaf cuttings. Seeds and offsets may also be used to cultivate them.

CHAPTER 4

Repotting Houseplants

Houseplants, which are once again fashionable, require repotting every year or two to stay stable and vigorous. Many of these plants emerge in the bleak rainforest floor, and although they've learned to deal with a lot of root rivalry, the confines of a pot will inevitably prove too much for them. Certain common houseplants, such as clivias, scheffleras, peace lilies, and ficus, prefer to be pot-bound, but still they may require repotting at some stage. It's the best time to do it now, at the outset of their annual growth cycle.

Apart from root congestion, plants that have been in a pot for so long are likely to be sitting in soil that has been compacted and polluted, as well as a dangerous buildup of fertilizer salts. When doing every sort of indoor plant treatment, including repotting, it's critical to examine each indoor plant individually.

The frequency of potting up (transplanting seedlings), repotting, or simply providing a soil adjustment is a significant factor that varies depending on the species and its condition. Repotting entails washing up, perhaps pruning roots, and replenishing soil, while 'potting up' refers to the process of transplanting seedlings.

The word 'potting on' is often used to describe transplanting to a larger pot.

HOW DO YOU TELL WHETHER A PLANT NEEDS REPOTTING?

Turn the pot over; roots coming out of the drainage holes is the most visible indicator of a pot-bound plant. Remove the plant's lower stem from the container with a tight grip. It's time to act if you see a thicket of pale roots in the form of the pot. If the pot won't come off, it's more likely due to clogged roots. You should take the jar out from the pot if it's made of plastic. If it's mud, you will need to use a hammer to smash it up.

Another symptom of a concern is whether the plant seems to be thirsty all of the time, wilting through regular watering. This is because the root-to-soil ratio has become too high. The same issue will result in a noticeable decrease in plant vigor.

To reduce the burden of the ordeal and make the roots more workable, water the plant deeply the day before repotting.

BENEFITS OF REPOTTING

The benefits of repotting for our indoor plants' health can be enormous. More space for plants to thrive, more air reaching the root system, preventing weak soil and roots from being root bound, resulting in loss of growth and waterlogged soil, more important nutrients provided, and disease prevention are only a few of the advantages.

WHEN TO REPOT

• ***Springtime***

Repotting is expected for the majority of indoor plants in the spring, and it's best done just before or when new growth appears. Because of the longer daylight hours, more heat, and warmer temperatures, this is a good time for new development.

Other plants on the other hands, like winter flowering species and bulbs that go dormant in the autumn, are not suitable for spring repotting. These plants should be repotted during fall. You should check the care directions for your specific plant.

TRUST ME: Check the quality and condition of all plants in the house at the start of the year.If you see that they need pruning, repotting, or some other kind of treatment, make a note of it for each plant. It's a fantastic way to prepare ahead of time. This is also a good time to prune if necessary.

• ***New Potted Plants***

Many house plants need to be repotted when they first get home, unless you feel they've been well cared for and the soil and pot size are right.

It's not rare to purchase plants that are in bad health, and need repotting. To avoid more shock from changes in the conditions and climate, repotting should be performed after a week or two of the plant settling into the house.

• ***Root/Pot bound***

When roots have outgrown their current pot, the word "root bound" or "pot bound" is used to indicate that it's time to try a larger pot. The classic 'roots growing through the drainage holes' and roots growing in a circular fashion since they have no space to expand, are signs of too much root for the pot. Keep in mind that certain plants, especially flowering varieties, benefit from a certain amount of close fitting inside a pot, which allows them to bloom more effectively (African violets are a good example).

You should remove the plant and see if it's pot bound from the outside of the pot if you're not sure. It won't hurt you, and you can return it until you've checked the roots.

• ***Plant or Pot Problems***

When a plant becomes pot bound, it may expand slowly or not at all. But first, check for underfeeding, overwatering, or a lack of light. Root bound can be identified by the soil drying out quickly.

When hard water is used or overfeeding is done, white ice-like forms on the outside edge of a clay pot, and a green slime forms as a result of blocked drainage or the plant being overwatered. Both would necessitate pot removal, potential repotting, fresh soil, and sterilization of the old pot.

STEPS OF REPOTTING

• ***Step 1 - Prepare the Pots***

It's a smart idea to scrub the pots thoroughly before sterilizing them with a 10% chlorine solution. This is done in order to keep plant pathogens at bay. It's worth giving terracotta pots a good soak for a couple of hours to eliminate the clay's dryness, allowing the fresh soil and plant to absorb as many of the nutrients as possible outside of the pot.

The controversy about whether to place terracotta, crock pieces, or other materials in the bottom of the pot has been with us since forever.

The biggest advantage of putting material in the bottom of a pot may be improved drainage and the avoidance of root rot caused by waterlogged soil. When a plant prefers to draw water from the bottom of the pot, where

there is no dirt, some farmers are afraid that insects may have better access to the plant (the bottom can have a small covering with tiny holes to solve this).
Plastic pots for plants that need a lot of drainage can benefit from crocking, and containers without drainage would need a layer of pebbles.

- ***Step 2 - Removing from the Pot***

Plants can be difficult to extract from containers, particularly if they've been root bound and have spent much time inside them. If everything else fails, crack the pot if it's clay or hack into plastic rather than yanking the plant out, which may cause major problems.

To remove soil from plastic potted plants, pressing the sides of the conta-iner gently loosens the soil, then turn the plant on its side and slip it out. Nine times out of ten, this will do. Clay potted plants can be more difficult to deal with as they cannot be squeezed. You may need to use a butter kni-fe to loosen them up by running it between the soil edge and the pot wall. If you're having trouble removing anything, look and see if any roots are emerging into the drainage holes. If this is the case, force them inward with a blunt object wider than the drainage hole or hack them out with a sharp knife.

TRUST ME: It's good to gently ease the plant out by keeping it at the bott-om of the stem with your hand in the dirt, but you must be very patient to know what plant you're dealing with. Woody and strong stems are easier, but some stems are so gentle you could snap your plant from the root ball easily.

Root Preparation: When the plant is out of its old container, inspect the root system and cut away any weakened or unnecessary roots. It is beneficial to remove some of the old dirt from the root ball. This is accomplished by massaging along the root ball's outer side and, in some cases, merely removing extra soil.

• *Step 3 - Fertilizer*

Fertilize the plant with a soluble all-purpose fertilizer that has been refined according to the label's instructions. Examine the plant to see if it needs repotting. Remember that once you've pruned the plant's leaves, it'll actually take less water than before, so change accordingly.
Within a week or two, you should see new development. Pinch out rising tips to facilitate branching until new shoots have two sets of leaves, then repeat on subsequent branches.

• *Step 4 - Potting*

When you've chosen a pot, washed it, selected the proper potting mix, and have a plant without a pot that's ready to be transplanted, just fill the bottom of the fresh pot with enough dirt.

When you can put the plant on top of the bottom soil with the plant stem and the beginning of the root segment sitting at the correct level with the rim of the container, you've got the right spot (allow a few millimeters or so gap below the rim for ease of watering).

It's time to fill in the margins, between the roots and the pot wall, until the location is right, and you're satisfied with the height the plant is sitting at.

It's helpful to gently drive your thumbs into the dirt, just don't overdo it and compact the soil to the point that air and water can't circulate freely. If future watering cause the soil to compress, you can still apply more top soil. You will not have enough root system to seat the plant after the first stage of filling the pot with soil. And that's perfect. Simply use the bottom soil to gauge the level and fill in the edges as best you can.

- ***Step 5 - Water, Care and Relax***

Now that you've completed the task, all that's left to do is to supply the repotted house plants with their favorite beverage: water. The majority of plants would need a thorough watering from the surface, allowing water to seep into the whole soil and root system, followed by 30 minutes of no additional water from the pot saucer. If the soil sinks too far after being watered, simply top it up.

When the plant is healing from the transplant, keep it out of direct sunlight and don't fertilizer for at least a month (new potting mix should have plenty of nutrients anyway).

Overwatering may cause sagging and limp leaves or roots, and if they turn yellow, you might be overwatering. You will relax as the plants absorb the new nutrients and thrive in their new space.

HOW TO PICK THE PERFECT POT

Have you ever believed you found the right pot for your houseplant, only to find it was completely wrong until you put it inside the container?

Plants are a kind of living being. Plants are delicate and have subtle characteristics that make them deserving of being the center of attention, and matching them with the right planters necessitates some consideration and preparation.

It may be difficult to ignore your beloved colors and patterns, but the colors and patterns you put on your body or paint on your walls will not be the same as the colours and patterns you see on the walls. Let's take a look at the fundamentals of selecting the best pots for our houseplants!

1. Hot Plants

Some plants have a vivid, shiny, and neon quality to them. Others have deep, rich tones that take center stage. Using neutral earth tones or monochromatic colours such as white, black, or grey can help to concentrate attention on your plants. These shades are also compatible with most home décor palettes, so you won't have to worry about clashing with your prized velvet emerald sofa! If you like bright colours, consider introducing colours that complement rather than clash with your plants.

2. Playful Patterns

Planting smaller houseplants in larger pots is a common mistake because certain plants grow slowly. Choose a plant pot that is the right size for the plant. Your smaller plants will tend to be larger and more full as a result of this!

3. Optical Illusions

Planting smaller houseplants in larger pots is a common mistake because certain plants grow slowly. Choose a plant pot that is the right size for the plant. Your smaller plants will tend to be larger and more full as a result of this!

4. Hang In There

Use vining plants to soften hard angles if you prefer tall, elongated planters. Unlike tall plants in tall plante-rs, which appear to project a stark, blunt focal point, the foliage will spill over the sides, forming a gentle wave.

CONCLUSION

Keeping indoor plants in decent physical condition is probably not the easiest of the hobbies, but taking care of such diverse, brautiful, happiness-gifting living beings can be the healthiest of the medicines for our everyday busy lives. This guide has been created with he aim to give you a no-fuss useful informations to give you an introduction to select some of the greatest green friends we could introduce into our homes.

All these plants can thrive indoors without a lot of light, air, or water. Indoor plants grow at a slower rate than those that grow outdoors and this allow us to keep them under control and make them be a nice addendum to our living spaces.

Of course you will have to make everything in your power to make your house a comfortable environment for them, for example keeping under check the air dryness. Especially during winter there may be a lack of moisture between the walls of our houses so we should help the plants keeping the humidity up or watering them more often, with chlorine-less water (just leave the tap-water in a bottle for a few days before using it to water your plants- and don't use the last bit of it).

Just using few precautions you can make your green thumb greener beef you can even realize it. I'd sugget you to start with your favorite two plant from this book. Just two, focus on them as they were your pets. Observe them and try to notice every little change in their shape, color, position, density, and adjust accordingly to their reaction. Observation is always the strongest tool when it comes to deal with another living being and plants are no different.

Give them some love and they will make your world a brighter place.

C.

INDEX

Printed in Great Britain
by Amazon